T0278977

THE SOCIAL LIFE
OF DEMOCRACY

THE INDIA LIST

THE SOCIAL LIFE OF DEMOCRACY

SUNDAR SARUKKAI

LONDON NEW YORK CALCUTTA

Seagull Books, 2022

First published by Seagull Books, 2022
© Sundar Sarukkai, 2022

ISBN   978 1 80309 174 7

British Library Cataloguing-in-Publication Data
A catalogue record for this book is available from the British Library

Typeset at Seagull Books, Calcutta, India
Printed and bound by WordsWorth India, New Delhi, India

'There cannot be democratic Government unless the society for which it functions is democratic in its form and structure.'

'If the mental disposition of the individuals is democratic then the democratic form of Government can be expected to result in good Government.'

Bhimrao R. Ambedkar
'Riddles in Hinduism'

CONTENTS

ACKNOWLEDGEMENTS

I am grateful to all those who have been part of, and who have supported, my attempts to bring philosophical thinking to different groups and domains. There is much that I have learned from Gopal Guru and I am deeply grateful for his intellectual support and personal *maitree*. Dhanu has been an onlooker in my struggles with democratic action in the everyday world and her critical gaze has helped my understanding of these issues on a practical plane; mere thanks are not enough for this lifelong learning. Bruce Kapferer has been a constant interlocutor and he has pushed my thinking beyond its safety zones—I cherish and acknowledge that engagement. Srinivasan Ramanujam has been my sounding board, particularly on Marxism and caste politics. I am indebted to him for this constant engagement as well as for his comments on the manuscript. Thanks are due to Amulya and Achintya, two young radicals, who taught me a lot about China and Communism, and although we would often end up in a heated debate it was always with a sense of friendly openness. My thanks also to my young nephew, Krishna, and younger niece, Sahana, who wanted to learn about Ambedkar and Marx, and through that process made me see how the new generation looks at old problems! Naveen Kishore at Seagull has been his usual gracious self and without his gentle nudging, this book would not have happened. I am grateful to him and his team for providing spaces for such reflections. Many thanks to Bishan Samaddar for his excellent editorial suggestions. Finally, my sense of gratitude to my parents who taught me through practice and not through theory the importance of living democratically in every sphere of my life and for showing in their own life practices how the vision of a social life of democracy is possible.

PREFACE

This long essay arose out of my attempts over the last many years to make philosophy meaningful to the public in India. One of the catalysts for this initiative, which also led me to start a forum called 'Barefoot Philosophers', was the polarization in public debates on many issues that mattered to our society, including religion, reservation, caste, gender and politics. In particular, I was deeply troubled by a pervasive belief, among people across the social spectrum, in the failure of Indian democracy. The suggestions to fix democracy from a range of groups varied from having military rule to having a government like in China and to inviting the British back to rule India! Many of these solutions have been bandied about in the public space and in private conversations. Although I found it amusing at first, I soon realized that too many of these responses were actually meant in all seriousness. Responding to the mood of the society, I wrote a series of newspaper op-eds and conducted workshops in philosophy for the public as well as children. That was obviously not enough, given the increasing polarization as well as the breakdown of dialogue between individuals and groups that held different views on various social issues. Hence, this long essay—some parts of which are based on my public writings as well as on experience drawn from my workshops— is an attempt to reach out and explain the conceptual basis of the uniqueness of democracy in India and to produce a more realistic and less ideological understanding of society, politics and democracy.

My unequivocal position is that democracy is essential to India. But what does democracy really mean? Today, in India, democracy for the public has been reduced to politics and a few rituals of elections and voting. If democracy is more than this, what could it be? The answers to this surround us, although they continue to be ignored. Two most insightful approaches to what democracy should be in India were given by Dr Bhimrao R. Ambedkar and Mohandas K. Gandhi. In my earlier work with Gopal Guru, we had discussed extensively the idea of the social that characterizes Indian reality as well as the philosophical foundations of caste. Rereading Ambedkar on democracy gave me an immediate framework for how I wanted to position my argument about democracy. I am convinced that Ambedkar's arguments about democracy, as something that are essentially related to mental dispositions and to the form of society, are extremely important. But how can we operationalize this important insight? This essay is an attempt to illustrate this possibility of a social life of democracy. This is not an essay on Ambedkar or a scholarly analysis of his ideas but his is the spirit which animates the arguments.

There is a huge amount of literature not only on democracy but also on Ambedkar. This book does not attempt to reproduce that style of academic scholarship, a style which I believe has led to the alienation of the public from engaging with the conceptual foundations of democracy. In the case of democracy, which is really about the people and the public, it is only apt that I communicate in a form that is accessible to, but yet challenges, them. So I have taken a middle path of avoiding excessive scholarship yet attempting to make my arguments as clear and rigorous as possible. It is not important whether the reader agrees with everything I say for I am more interested in whether it catalyses their critical thinking about their own assumptions about democracy.

The aim of this book is to understand what it means for each one of us to be more democratic in our day-to-day actions and less about how governments can be democratic. It is an attempt to discover, following Ambedkar's observation, the obstacles, the possibilities and the way to achieve democracy as a form of society based on mental dispositions rather than merely as a form of governance. It is a reflection on how we can produce our own democratic selves. The first step towards this possibility lies in having conceptual clarity of the many terms that are associated with democracy. Thus, it is an exploration of how each of us can act democratically rather than reduce democracy as judgement on how others—the government, institutions and leaders, for instance—should act. I believe that this is the most important lesson that we can get from Ambedkar's views on democracy. After all, Ambedkar's argument that political democracy is not possible without social democracy necessitates finding ways to produce a social democracy based on the ideas of liberty, equality and fraternity. My argument is that this form of social democracy is possible only through the cultivation of a democratic self as well as critically understanding the broad range of concepts that are nested within the idea of democracy that should be part of public discourses and not produced exclusively within academic ones. These steps are necessary if democracy has to have a meaningful future.

1.

THE NATURE OF DEMOCRACY

India is the world's largest democracy and yet when we travel across the breadth of the nation it would be difficult to find a cohesive understanding or homogenous experiences of democracy among the people. Even within the political space of elections, most of the ideas surrounding democracy as articulated by scholars seem to be absent in the consciousness of a large number of citizens. To say that India is the largest democracy is only in name, only in a quantitative sense of the numbers who vote. It is not only that there is a dearth of democratic actions in the daily life of the people, in their interactions with government agencies and with private business, or when they engage with social spaces like hospitals, it is also that there is a lack of expectation of the ideals of democracy. Social relations are still mediated by various exclusionary structures including caste, class, gender and religion. Most of rural India is partitioned along these lines and increasingly it is happening in the urban areas too. In many rural areas, people are quite indifferent to who the 'rulers' in Delhi are since their world revolves around their daily lives, daily survival and everyday cultural practices.

Democracy cannot be reduced only to the political space, to governments that are elected. It is now more important than ever to recollect Ambedkar's important insight that democracy is a 'form of the organization of the society' and that it is impossible to think of democracy if the society itself is not democratic.[1] Democracy is not politics alone but a 'philosophy of life', and the success of it is possible only if the 'mental disposition of the individuals is democratic.'[2] Scholars have pointed out that Ambedkar's description of democracy is deeply influenced by the words of his teacher, John Dewey, who wrote that 'A democracy is more than a form of government; it is primarily a mode of associated living, of conjoint communicated experience.'[3] There is an important difference in the wording of both Dewey and Ambedkar. If Dewey focuses on 'associated living', Ambedkar stresses on the organization of the society since the challenge to Indian society is the possibility of associated living.[4]

For Ambedkar, the way to democracy is through the three values of the French revolution: liberty, equality and fraternity. But he also argues that equality and liberty are not enough and what sustains them, and thus any idea of democracy, is fraternity. As he notes, 'If in Democracy liberty does not destroy equality and equality does not destroy liberty, it is because at the basis of both there is fraternity. Fraternity is therefore the

---

1 See B. R. Ambedkar, 'Riddles in Hinduism'. See also Scott Stroud, 'Pragmatist Riddles in Ambedkar's "Riddles of Hinduism"', *Forward Press*, 1 June 2019. Available at https://bit.ly/3Q2sfME (last accessed on 20 June 2022).

2 Ambedkar, 'Riddles in Hinduism', pp. 282–3.

3 John Dewey, *The Middle Works of John Dewey, 1899–1924; Volume 9: 1916, Democracy and Education* (Jo Ann Boydston ed.) (Carbondale and Edwardsville: Southern Illinois University Press), p. 93.

4 See Arun P. Mukherjee, 'B. R. Ambedkar, John Dewey, and the Meaning of Democracy', *New Literary History* 40(2) (2009): 345–70.

root of Democracy.'[5] It is this larger sense of fraternity that he names *Maitree*.

Thus, the prescription seems clear. Without fraternity within a society, there is no possibility of democracy. But what is it to have fraternity in a society? What are the conceptual and pragmatic obstacles to the realization of this project? What Ambedkar points out seems so obvious and true but then why has it not been taken seriously and operationalized? Even if it is the case that democracy has been reduced to a particular kind of political action, what kind of thinking and action is required to mould democracy to this vision? Ambedkar, in the last speech to the Constituent Assembly as the Chair of the Drafting Committee, observed that the challenge for the newly independent India was to retain its democracy. He offered three suggestions: holding 'fast to constitutional methods', not allowing hero-worship of its leaders, and recognizing that political democracy is not enough. With regard to the last suggestion, he notes that 'Political democracy cannot last unless there lies at the base of it social democracy. What does social democracy mean? It means a way of life which recognizes liberty, equality and fraternity as the principles of life.'[6]

How does one understand democracy in order to discover in it not merely some ideas of political representation but fraternity in society? If democracy needs the individual's 'mental disposition' to be democratic, then what should the ideal processes of democracy be? How does a society produce this mental disposition? This essay is an attempt to describe the obstacles

---

5 Ambedkar, 'Riddles in Hinduism', pp. 283.

6 B. R. Ambedkar, *Dr. Babasaheb Ambedkar: Writings and Speeches, Volume 13* (Vasant Moon ed.) (Mumbai: Education Department, Government of Maharashtra, 1994), pp. 1215–16.

and challenges in achieving these goals of democracy. It is a very small step in discovering the possibility of implementing this vision of thinkers and leaders like Ambedkar and Gandhi.

Such a project is possible only by beginning with the experiences of democracy. These experiences are structured through a certain conceptual understanding of the various elements of democracy. Thus, a core aim of this essay is to reflect on these conceptual foundations of democracy as we see it in practice in places like India in order to make sense of the experience of democracy by its people. This exercise about democracy is one way to establish my firm conviction that the only way democracy can function effectively is if it becomes part of our daily lives and not remain as an isolated set of acts related to politics. It is in this sense that I invoke the term 'social life of democracy' to suggest that democracy should always be understood in the context of its social life. We repeatedly hear that strengthening democracy is to strengthen its institutions and the system of elections but what is most needed now is the strengthening of the life of democracy in individuals and in everyday social practices. But what are the obstacles to this vision? Why cannot we produce a society that is democratic? My attempt to address these questions does not aim to producing normative answers but to examine how we need to understand the various ideas that are needed to produce this possibility of a democratic society.

I will begin by exploring the conceptual basis of democracy and analyse what needs to be done to this conceptual understanding in order to move towards democracy as a way of life and not just as a periodic ritual. What conceptual clarity do we need in order to make sense of the claim that democracy is social organization? So what I will do through the length of this essay is to work with some foundational concepts related to democracy such as People, Voting, Freedom, Truth and so on. I will explore the topography of these concepts so that we understand what conditions need to be fulfilled if democracy has to be a part of our daily lives. This approach is in no way a scholarly work on Ambedkar nor on the legal and constitutional contributions to democracy by Ambedkar. It is an attempt to fill out the contours of Ambedkar's social imagination of democracy and is driven by the spirit of Ambedkar's observations on democracy and society. What follows can be read as an attempt to see how such a vision is possible as well as the obstacles to such a vision in the contemporary context.

The fundamental paradox about democracy is that it has rhetorically invested so much in the idea of 'the People'. However, critics of democracy also point out that it is 'the People' who are also the problem many a time. For democracy in some parts of the West, the notion of 'the People' is a normative idea of the unity of their citizens. In India, we have to find the proper articulation of what it means for all of us to belong to one 'People'. For many reasons, not least of which is the linguistic differences in almost every state in the country, the gelling of citizens into People has not happened. The recent attempts to bully people of different castes and religions to follow uniform norms of behaviour are a reflection of the continued attempt to produce this category of 'the People'. Democracy as a political act gifts freedom to every adult to vote but as a social process it has continued to look down upon the common voter. People are the backbone of political democracy but are also the ones who are most reviled, abused and manipulated. At its conceptual heart, there is a problem with our democracy.

So it is not a surprise that democracy is in a crisis. Not only are blatant expressions of anti-democratic sentiment growing around the world, but there are also attempts to expand and dilute the definitions of democracy, thereby eroding its value. Part of the problem confronting democracy is that the idea of democracy itself has not been democratically positioned. Firstly, the hegemony and hierarchy of values that define democracy of the major democratic powers have alienated a significant part of the world that is not included in a small group comprising of the US, UK, Germany, etc. Secondly, the restriction of democracy to purely matters of politics has led to a conceptual dilution, whereby this idea gets too closely aligned to characteristics of power that is central to politics. Thirdly, the theoretical work on democracy repeatedly betrays the undemocratic relationship between theory produced by members of the academic community and the experience of the 'laypeople'. The fact that very little of the theoretical work from Asia and Africa enters into the global mainstream discourse on democracy exemplifies the inherent lack of democracy in academics today as well as the undemocratic relationship between the scholars and 'the People'. The fundamental question that we should be asking is not whether nations have democratic rule but what it is to live a democratic life. It is the focus on living the democratic life that will save whatever value that different notions of democracy possess. Democracy is a lifeworld and has to be part of our lived experience of our everyday lives. This is the only guarantee for the survival of democracy.

India is often described as the world's largest democracy, although this has recently been challenged by the Chinese. We are also repeatedly told that democracy in India is not in an ideal shape. Seeing what is happening in parliaments and legislatures, seeing the rampant and blatant corruption and misuse of power—selling of votes and so on—one can understand why it is said that Indian democracy is in a crisis. But this conclusion has been arrived at a bit too quickly. If democracy is seen to be limited to certain political processes, then, yes, there is a moment of crisis that needs to be addressed. However, the mistake is also in thinking of democracy in this manner. Instead, if democracy is understood as a form of life, then we can immediately see that there are forms of democratic life that are present in so many parts of society even if not among the ruling political elite. It is this democracy as a form of life that needs to be strengthened and not be allowed to get lost in a narrow vision of democracy driven by models of democracy drawn from elsewhere.

Today, democracy has to be thought of differently. Earlier analyses focused too much on certain concepts underlying democracy as well as institutional structures. Later, civil society as a conceptual term began to gain importance. However, the transformations in democracy today are also deeply influenced by the technological changes in our societies. Much has been made of the influence of social media on so-called democratic movements like the Arab Spring. However, such conclusions focus on the product of technologies and not on the nature of these technologies which are transforming the institutional character of democracy.

Institutions of democracy have been essential for sustaining it in any country. However, they were also gatekeepers. The participation of 'People' was always at a distance and through others who represented them. Gradually, even visiting these institutions became impossible due to various security measures. Sociologically, institutions retained their prominence in any analysis of democracy but they were also abstract as far as democracy qua individuals was concerned. In a pre-digital world, freedom of expression was largely reduced to freedom of the press. But as any member of the common public knew well, it was also impossible to be a part of the press, to get individual opinions published. There was always the fourth wall in journalism, like in theatre. And more powerfully so in politics itself. In India, like in some other places, politics is more of a performance. It is staged in every sense of the word. So the people become the audience to the performance of politics, and politicians perform as if there is an invisible fourth wall between them and the audience.

What digital technology and social media have done is make some of the institutional structures redundant. Print media struggles to survive not just because of material changes but also because of the surplus of people in social media writing about issues which were earlier the sole domain of journalists. This does not mean that social media and its associated technologies promote democracy; rather, what they primarily have done is to change the meaning of representation and in a sense have brought the possibility of democracy into their lives. It makes possible new experiences of democracy—one unfortunate consequence is the free spewing of hate. Most importantly, in this digital world democracy will be radically questioned because it claims to bring the experiences of democracy literally into each individual's palms. However, any claim that these technologies increase the possibility of producing democracy will be short-lived since the technologies are produced in a regime of secrecy and are closely related to hegemonic power. We are now witnessing the use of these technologies in far more repressive ways by powerful governments rather than in a revolution towards true democracy.

The political life of democracy does not reach most people in our country. They live oblivious of who the government is, what they do and how it should affect their lives. For some of them, the government in Delhi is as alien as the Britishers when they ruled the country. Democracy as a form of politics does not touch the citizens. On average, 40 to 50 per cent of the people who have the right to vote do not vote. It does not make sense to thus declare countries as democratic or not based on this voting system. In contrast, there is an experience of democracy that can be part of our everyday lives. What this suggests is that democracy, if it has to have any meaningful value, has to be seen to be part of our social lives. A political life of democracy is not only incomplete but also impossible without a social life of democracy. In what follows, I want to explore the contours of this social life of democracy.

2.

THE CONCEPT OF DEMOCRACY

It is remarkable that we hear so many complaints that we in India do not live in a democracy although we are often touted as the biggest democratic nation in the world. In every sphere, including politics, the first line of criticism seems to be that we are not 'really' a democracy. In recent times, US president Donald J. Trump was often accused of trying to destroy democratic institutions, and similar charges are heard repeatedly about the BJP government today.

On the other hand, we routinely hear claims from countries like China, which is seen as 'non-democratic' by the international community, that they too are democratic. As recently as December 2021, the Chinese government released a report on why China is a democracy. What makes these multiple narratives about democracy possible is the ambiguous meaning of democracy. In the global world, the USA is often seen as the beacon of democracy, a view that drives not just its internal politics but also its external interventions as a 'safe-guarder' of democracy in other societies. India's claim has recently been challenged by China when it declared itself the world's largest democracy based on the number of people who participated in its local elections. There are other governments which do not fit the American model of democracy but call themselves so. There are countries with monarchies, with military rule, with one-man totalitarian rule, all of which call themselves democracies. Most often the term democracy is itself qualified in various ways, such as people's democracy, direct democracy, participative democracy, presidential democracy, parliamentary democracy, etc. The idea of culture-specific democracies has become quite popular, especially in Asia. So we hear of the uniqueness of 'Indian democracy', 'Chinese democracy', 'Asian democracies' and 'African democracies'. What is really common to all these democracies? Is the use of the word 'democracy' a rhetorical move given the geopolitical value that has accrued to this concept? Or are the multiple descriptions a subtle way of challenging colonizing descriptions of democracy?

These descriptions of democracy pose some fundamental challenges to the idea of a Western democracy, a term that Asian democracies position themselves against. The argument is that Western democracy is a particular model that is not sensitive to the cultures of other parts of the world. Equivalently, what this also implies is that Western democracy is itself premised on the culture of Western societies, at least those that see themselves as upholding this model of democracy. Such a claim is not unreasonable. People in a society are influenced by their cultural beliefs and they act based on those beliefs as well as their understanding of concepts such as the social, government, leadership, governance, responsibility, duty and so on. In India, the family plays an important social role in so many aspects of an individual's life. So it is not a surprise to note that the family is deeply ingrained in democratic politics. But this does not mean that we have to accept established practices as culturally predetermined and unchangeable. As a society, one might desire other systems of politics and governance that are more like democracy in other countries. But to do this we have to first acknowledge that the idea of democracy is itself based on specific cultural beliefs about many fundamental concepts including those of 'individual', 'people', 'freedom', 'responsibility', 'governance' and so on.

When we commonly use the term 'democracy', we might be referring to different characteristics. One might be talking about democracy as a purely political process whereas another might be using the word to imply equality. Democracy, like all concepts, has varied meanings. It is generally the case that a concept's meaning is given by the context in which it is used; when a group of people talk about that concept they may not mean the same thing. Even a term like 'religion' will have different senses when used in different contexts and by different people. For example, I might be using the word religion as something to do with a religious text, whereas the person who is responding to me might be using the same word as a set of beliefs related to faith. Another might use the word to refer to a set of practices in relation to a supernatural being called god. Thus, the conflict that we have in private and public discourse is not as much about the meanings of concepts as it is about the human tendency to use the same words with very different meanings. We often talk at cross-purposes without recognizing that we do so. Concepts such as equality, oppression, rights, democracy, justice, like almost every other concept that is part of our social life, are filled with these multiple meanings and multiple senses. So before discussing what democracy is and what it could be, one of the first things that we need to do is delineate the different meanings of this word.

The most common meaning of democracy is as a political system. The commonly translated meaning of this term is 'power of the people', 'rule of the people'. This idea seems simple enough: people belonging to a group should have a say in how the group should be governed and 'ruled', who has the power to take decisions and so on. This etymology has overly influenced the meaning of democracy and restricted it primarily to the domain of governance, power and politics. But like all influential words, this word begins to be used in other contexts and picks up different meanings. As we saw above, some of the common phrases associated with this word include the following: representative democracy, direct democracy, liberal democracy, participatory democracy, parliamentary democracy, social democracy, grassroots democracy. In our everyday talk, we often refer to undemocratic practices of institutions, schools, hospitals; children who begin to use this word do so when they are upset about being denied something and say that their parents are not being democratic. Democracy, as a general term, has a valency that allows this migration into other domains quite easily because there is something about democracy that is always more than politics.

First of all, even if democracy is understood as 'power/rule of the people', terms such as 'power', 'rule' and 'people' are themselves quite ambiguous. The different meanings of democracy are put loosely under the concept of democracy because of the different meanings of these terms. In so doing, we can see why the claim that democracy is a Western notion, with its origin located among the ancient Greeks, needs to be re-examined. The first conceptual challenge lies in the idea of 'the People'. It is not very different from the challenge of interpreting the powerful phrase 'We, the People', embedded in the preamble of the Indian Constitution and other democratic systems. The term 'People' refers to a collective. How do we define who 'the People' are? Are they the elite in society? Are they the ones who are 'eligible' to vote? Are they the educated ones? Do people of all sections, including the marginalized, women and children, have an equal belonging to this group called 'the People'? Are 'foreigners' part of this group? This confusion is at the heart of many ambiguous, counter-claims about democracy and the reasons for its failure in many cases. This has been exacerbated by the repeated invocation of the popular expression that describes democracy as 'Of the people, By the people, For the people'. This phrase appears in Abraham Lincoln's Gettysburg Address and it is instructive to see the line in which it is used: '. . . that these dead shall not have died in vain—that this nation, under god, shall have a new birth of freedom and that government of the people, by the people, for the people shall not perish from the earth'.[1] It is instructive to note that the birth of this phrase, so famously associated with democracy, could not go beyond a limited view of the term 'people', since it excluded the original inhabitants of that country as well as Black people and women in most democratic processes that followed, including voting.

So the first challenge in understanding democracy, even in this restricted political sense of governance, is to define the parameters for this group called 'the People'. One could say that all 'citizens' are 'the People'. But that is not true since there are many people living in a society who may be part of it but not citizens of it. Moreover, in many countries, citizenship itself is a contentious claim and depends on the State granting them this privilege. The problem also lies in the use of the word 'we'. Who is this 'we'? Is it a mere collection of individuals? Collections can be referred to in other ways too, such as 'they' and 'them'. 'We' and 'us' are specific qualities of a collection of people. The way we use these terms suggests a particular type of relationship—a form of belonging perhaps—in the collection.

---

1 Abraham Lincoln, 'Gettysburg Address', delivered at Gettysburg, Pennsylvania, 19 November 1863. Available at: https://bit.ly/3KJpQ7m (last accessed on 2 September 2022).

It is a collection that includes the 'individual', the speaking subject, the 'I'. When I use the words 'we' or 'us', I am including myself in that group. When I use 'they', I am explicitly keeping myself out of the group.

Thus, to understand the meaning of 'we' it is necessary to understand the meaning of 'I' and the relation between 'we' and 'I', the collective and the self. Any attempt to understand the nature of democracy has to begin with this relationship between the self and the collective. Given that different cultures have different meanings of the self and the collective, it is reasonable to believe that the articulations of democracy will be different in different cultures. For example, in India, family is a dominant social force and has become integral to Indian politics. Family members retain power in political parties and there are innumerable examples of families continuing to hold power in the various states. Even the BJP's claim to power was partly based on an attack on the dynastic policy of the Congress. But all parties in India have continued to promote their own family members in politics. A major reason for the lack of response from the people to such obvious manipulation lies in the way the self is understood within the various social groups in India. Whatever be their religion or caste, the self is to a great extent subsumed within the family. The family still takes decisions on some of the most important aspects of an individual's growth including their education plans, job choices and decision on their spouses.

The 'we' can be defined in various ways: legally in being granted citizenship to a nation, socially through membership to groups and institutions, through concepts such as the public, as a set of experiences that groups share, as a feeling of togetherness. The sense of 'we' can be produced through recognition of cultural similarities, religious beliefs or secular principles. There are specific mechanisms that can produce the possibility of a 'we'. For example, right at the beginning of the formation of a country like the United States, a covenant was the basis of defining 'We, the People'. This document was grounded in religious thought and invoked 'a higher moral basis' to enforce certain types of behaviour.[2] The possibility of a community based on such a covenant supplied the 'principles and guidelines' to form the rules of a moral society, and a Constitution is the 'written, "operational" form of a covenant' which allows the principles of community formation to continue.[3] The American Declaration of Independence expressing the covenant was seen by Lincoln as the document which would create a national identity for that country based on principles of learning to live together. But it is important to note that the need for such a covenant was based on a particular understanding of the nature of human beings, dominantly as those who are caught between being selfish and working to benefit others. Right from the beginning, the American vision of democracy was built on ideas of institutionalizing these principles of the covenant and finding principles to address the assumed innate selfishness of human individuals. One can immediately see that this approach to the formation of a community is based on a specific cultural understanding of an individual and the nature of the relationship between individuals. It is a particular way of understanding our existence. So the idea of covenant and democracy based on the creation of a community are premised on assumptions about the nature of

---

2 Emily Gray, '"Of the People, By the People, For the People": The Implications of Covenantal Union for the Legitimacy of Secession in the United States' (New Haven, CT: Department of Political Science, Yale University, 2013), p. 4. Available at: https://bit.ly/3RomuK7 (last accessed on 9 July 2022).

3 Gray, 'Of the People', p. 5.

human beings—as being selfish and only working for one's benefit. But is this a universal trait of humans? Are there other ways to understand the nature of humans? The possibility that other cultures conceive of humans and human relations in different ways immediately opens up the possibility that some fundamental ideas of democracy—based on harmonious community existence as well as allowing for individual liberty—can in principle be different in different cultures. The above example is useful in isolating the originary impulse in modern democracy which was really not about representation and rule as it was about the possibility of producing a harmonious and free community. This quality illustrates one aspect of what I mean by the social life of democracy, the fact that democracy is much more than some political action but corresponds to basic practices that create a sense of a harmonious social.

The American case is different from most other societies in that they had the 'freedom' to imagine a new society since they were forming such a society from the flow of immigrants from Europe. In contrast, at the time the Americas were yet to be conquered by the Europeans, Asian societies like India and China had already well-established social orders. This major difference in the nature of these societies has an impact on how we understand the functions of democracy in these countries. The difference between articulating democratic ideals (which are also based on ideals of sociality) in the American case and those of already stratified societies (not just in Asia but also in Europe) challenges any naive comparison between the democratic systems and processes between these countries. But if the spirit of democracy is the search for principles that can form a harmonious society and can produce a sense of we-ness among its people, then we can discover democracy in different societies by articulating these principles. These are the principles which bring together people to live in a mode of coexistence and where individual action is also directed towards the benefit of others in that community. When democracy is understood in this manner, the central claim of Ambedkar about the nature of democracy naturally follows.

It is not that there were no governing principles, including moral ones, that ordered these well-stratified societies like in India and China. Not all these cultures base their social principles on a fundamental suspicion of the human individual, nor are they driven by a particular belief (modernist?) in the innate selfishness of individuals. As an example, we could consider the possibility of producing a society governed through the ideas of self-governance. An excessive emphasis on democracy as governance 'by a few, for the many' has led to the erasure of one of the most important principles of democracy, namely, the governance of the self. Democratic principles have to first begin with the self in its various actions. If there is anything that we can learn from democratic movements in Asia and India, in particular, it is this emphasis on the self as the locus of democratic action. A democracy built around these principles of the self will have quite different characteristics compared with cultures where the individual is defined through freedom of a particular kind. In the case of democracy built around the idea of the governing self, democracy becomes a part of everyday life and is not necessarily exemplified through actions that place a great emphasis on certain notions of individual freedom. This is a foundational tension that lies at the heart of democracy that is based on attempts to produce a harmonious society of 'free' individuals. In the case of India and Africa, it was necessary to discover the domain of individual freedom since social structures were already well established, and these structures were to the detriment of various caste and gender groups. So if

American democracy arose as an attempt to produce the possibility of a new society from disparate individuals, democracy in Asia struggled to find ways to maintain or modify the existing society by acknowledging new ideas of 'free' individuals. This difference and contradiction lie at the root of competing claims about the nature of democracy in different societies around the world. The complexity of this difference also lies in certain foundational problems in the idea of freedom itself, a topic that I will address at the end of this book.

The emphasis on a simplistic idea of individual freedom (which today is little more than the idea of 'consumer choice') as the basis of building a community is at its heart contradictory unless the nature of the individual self is clearly understood. It is contradictory not because of beliefs that humans are inherently selfish and would not, given a chance, do anything for the benefit of others but because the conceptions of a freely acting self have been constructed in a manner that promotes this view. Societies in which there are different conceptions of the social have different approaches to the role of the self in relation to the community. This does not mean that these approaches are better as far as the individual is concerned but it is this instability around different performative functions of the self in everyday life that produces confusion about democracy. We could say that today democracy is failing all around us because as individuals, we have put the burden of being democratic onto other structures. We think democracy is something we inherit and that others have to do the job of being democratic. Governments, political parties and institutions are expected to be democratic. But how can they be so when as individuals we do not know what it is to be democratic and how to be democratic? This question can lead us to better understand Ambedkar's view on democracy in its relation to society.

Both in practice and theory, democracy in India is different from democracy in other nations. Although India is often grouped along with those nations that are seen as the flag-bearers of democracy such as the US, England, France, Germany etc., there are nevertheless fundamental differences in the way democracy operates in India as well as in the theoretical implications of its democracy. In a sense, this difference reflects arguments of the proponents of 'Asian democracies' about the cultural influence on the idea of democracy and the resistance to accepting one particular model of democracy driven by certain Western nations. Interestingly, Ambedkar points out that the idea of democracy was not alien to India. It is important to read his observation in full:

> There was a time when India was studded with republics, and even where there were monarchies, they were either elected or limited. They were never absolute. It is not that India did not know Parliaments or Parliamentary Procedure. A study of the Buddhist Bhikshu Sanghas discloses that not only there were Parliaments—for the Sanghas were nothing but Parliaments—but the Sanghas knew and observed all the rules of Parliamentary Procedure known to modern times. They had rules regarding seating arrangements, rules regarding Motions, Resolutions, Quorum, Whip, Counting of Votes, Voting by Ballot, Censure Motion, Regularization, Res Judicata, etc. Although these rules of Parliamentary Procedure were applied by the Buddha to the meetings of the Sanghas, he must have borrowed them from the rules of the Political Assemblies functioning in the country in his time.[4]

---

4 Ambedkar, *Writings and Speeches, Volume 13*, pp. 1214–15.

Ambedkar rues the fact that these forms of democracy had been lost and cautions against losing democracy again. His worry was well grounded if we look at what political democracy has become in India today. At the ground level, democracy in India exhibits many characteristics that seem to be undemocratic. First of all, democracy has been reduced to a ritual of elections and voting. And even this, too, is imperfect—voters are offered inducements and, many times, money. That this happens openly and is acknowledged freely by political parties as well as voters merely indicates a deep sense of indifference to core principles of democracy. Moreover, none of the political parties allow for democratic practices in their own internal governance. Families and individuals dominate parties. Blatant corruption by elected politicians is endemic and there is little attempt to even counter it. Democracy in institutions is not seen as a prerequisite for political democracy. The fruits of democracy do not reach the poorest and the disadvantaged. Do these characteristics of Indian democracy point to a problem with democracy or does it suggest that we need a different approach to democracy in a place like India? Or does it only point to a bird's eye view of democracy without understanding how it could be functioning through a different register at the lower levels of society?

On the surface, democracy in India appears to have the problems listed above, and perhaps it is because of this that global discourse on democracy ignores the ideas and possibilities of deriving lessons about it from India and other non-Western nations. In a comprehensive document on democracy in India, political scientist K. C. Suri, points out:

> What is surprising is that, by and large, the global debates and theorization on democracy go on as if India's democracy does not matter, even though it is

the world's most populous democracy with more than one-third of the population living in democracies [being] in India. [...] In the standard textbooks and reference books on theories of democracy, India and Indian thinkers hardly figure.[5]

This observation is not particularly surprising given that non-Western nations have primarily become the fodder of empirical data for theorists from outside these countries. The myth that somehow the idea of democracy is intrinsic to the West and is antithetical to Asia, Middle East and Africa has been constantly perpetuated and is strengthened by the claim that democracy's exclusive origin is Greek thought. Given the predominance of a theoretical discourse being driven by the cultural specificities of Western nations who see themselves as the flag bearers of democracy, it is not surprising that there is a greater urgency to 'institutionalize democracy'. Suri suggests that a 'more useful way of understanding democracy in any country is to see it as a process where the values and institutions of democracy grow and consolidate, where the goalpost keeps moving farther as a country makes progress.'[6] Contrasting this with democracy as a form of social organization, we can see that locating democracy exclusively within institutions reflects a suspicion towards individuals and the communities they form based on differing associative patterns, including caste and religion. While this step is extremely important and necessary, it is not sufficient to produce a democratic social as the first step of democracy.

---

5 K. C. Suri, 'India's Democracy—An Exception or a Model?' in K. C. Suri and Achin Vanaik (eds), *Political Science, Volume 2: Indian Democracy* (New Delhi: Oxford Scholarship Online, 2013), p. 3.

6 Suri, 'India's Democracy', p. 5.

In an excellent overview of Indian democracy, Neera Chandhoke and Rajesh Kumar too point out one important consequence of institutionalization. They suggest that the 'one outstanding achievement of Indian democracy has been the institutionalization of political equality'.[7] But they also argue that democracy's function must be through civil society, a term that moves towards the social but is still within the orbit of institutions since the civil society as a concept in India is itself fractured. When we extend the move from civil society to the everyday social, the chances of creating a democratic society increase. Chandhoke and Kumar would also like to see Indian democracy not as a fixed point but as one that is emerging and that can function as a model for other democracies.

There are some general patterns that scholars have identified as being unique to Indian democracy which in major part explain its success. Some of the leading successes are: (1) the impact that democratic politics has had on social structure, such as the loosening of the rigid caste structure of traditional societies; (2) giving a sense of agency to the poor and the economic and social non-elite; (3) the defining of the most visible aspect of politics through identity formation based on caste and religion rather than on community interests alone.[8] What has often been pointed out is the fact that historically it is the poor

---

7 Neera Chandhoke and Rajesh Kumar, 'Indian Democracy: Cognitive Maps' in K. C. Suri and Achin Vanaik (eds), *Political Science, Volume 2: Indian Democracy* (New Delhi: Oxford Scholarship Online, 2013), p. 19.

8 Chandhoke and Kumar, 'Indian Democracy', p. 21. See also Sanjay Reddy, 'A Rising Tide of Demands: India's Public Institutions and the Democratic Revolution' in Devesh Kapur and Pratap B. Mehta (eds), *Public Institutions in India: Performance and Design* (New Delhi: Oxford University Press, 2005), pp. 457–75. For a political theory of Indian democracy, see D. L. Sheth, *At Home with Democracy: A Theory of Indian Politics* (Singapore: Palgrave Macmillan, 2018).

and the poorer classes that have participated in voting. The elite's participation in voting and elections in general has been comparatively less. This has also meant a major shift in the focus of politicians, one that almost exclusively addresses the non-elite in the public domain. Javeed Alam argues that it is through politics that the poor and the socially disadvantaged find a space of equality, or at least potential equality.[9] Thus, participation in politics is more a surrogate for a social movement for equality. Although this process is a movement towards the Ambedkarite vision of democracy, it is still incomplete and will remain so, given the nature of the vehicle that moves towards social equality. Alam argues that it is this group of 'ordinary people' that protects democracy, or at least democracy as understood in a more limited sense: as political participation leading to experiences of social equality rather than as a set of rules that govern institutional practices. What these observations by Alam and other scholars show is that Indian democracy should be seen first as a social process rather than as a political one. Here, one might question this emphasis on the difference between the social and the political. I think it is clear that the uniqueness of Indian democracy these scholars point to is also representative of the uniqueness of the Indian social, one that is not duplicated in other liberal democracies.

In response, Chandhoke and Kumar argue that while this aspiration of the non-elites is important, it is the impact of these aspirations on democratic institutions that is noteworthy. They point out that politics in India has been instrumental in gener-ating identities, particularly on caste lines, and extends the idea of the right of individuals to the right of groups. Expanding the notion of democracy, along with freedom, they add participation,

---

9 Javeed Alam, *Who Wants Democracy?* (Hyderabad: Orient Longman, 2006).

competition and accountability as democratic qualities, which, they note, have all improved.[10] But problems in institutional settings related to law and governance have had mixed effects. What characterizes Indian democracy is the constant confusion between individual and group identities. Democratic qualities such as freedom are meaningful as individual action but the social order which produces the constant conflict between the individual and the social has a debilitating effect on democracy that is overly based on the notions of autonomy and freedom of the individual. What is democracy in a society in which the individual herself is a deeply social being? What does the notion of freedom mean for a person who has a dominant group identity? The individual is actually instrumentalized in democracies where there is a constant intermingling of the individual and the social. The individual is only present at the moment of voting as an individual. But till she reaches the voting booth and as soon as she is out of the booth, she functions as a member of a social group that dominates her actions. Even in voting, this contradiction is manifested because in many cases, one does not vote for oneself but only for and on behalf of others such as their caste or religious group.

In other words, political society has succeeded in institutionalizing personal lives of people to the extent that families, caste and religious identity have all become part of politics. Thus, it is not a surprise that political institutions are deeply integrated with social institutions; caste identities are institutionalized in the 'headquarters' of various caste groups, and so also in the case of institutional religion. These cultural and social institutions have a deep hold on the political process not just by their proximity to the rulers but by their capacity to convert

---

10 Chandhoke and Kumar, 'Indian Democracy', p. 30.

individual voting to a process of group voting. The family has entered the political in almost every political party that we see in India; through this action, an institutionalization of the family also takes place.

But the instrumentalization of the voter also leads to the instrumentalization of the politician. Extracting payment for voting for a particular candidate is one such example. Political positions, such as chief ministership, ministership or even getting a party ticket to contest elections, are most often determined on the basis of payment by the individual to the party. These practices have become so professional and institutionalized that political parties do this effortlessly and seamlessly. They come up with various ways to do this while recognizing that their actions may often border on the illegal. Ironically, it is only in the payment for votes that a voter is really seen as an individual, since the money is given to each of them. Even when he or she votes, there is no individuality since voting is often done as a bloc based on the payments. In many poorer communities, it is not that a politician actually engages with each individual. Each of these communities, defined by the place they live in or the low-income housing that they might occupy, usually has a 'leader' or a middleman. It is the leader who is the mediator and who is also the guarantor to the politician. In such cases, individuals who get money to vote for a particular politician are doing so on the instructions of the 'leader' of their group. Such practices may seem to be far removed from an ideal vision of individual freedom and autonomy but these notions are 'ideal' precisely for the reason that they are alien to the social world in which these people live. Most significantly, negotiation with their leader and the politician becomes part of their daily lives, and in this sense politics enters their household much more intimately than anonymous institutions.

One of the ideals of democracy is equality, another term which has attained enough ambiguity in this context and has thus become associated with a restricted set of meanings, such as the equal right to vote. Extremely unequal populations simulate equality only at the moment of voting. They come from their unequal social reality and go back to it after the vote. Access to democratic institutions is also very unequal and those who are economically and socially well off get differential access to what should be available equally to all. Chandhoke and Kumar are aware of this and therefore propose that 'democracy can only be realized when political equality helps us realize social and economic equality'.[11] But this is also precisely the problem since political democracy continues without demanding social and economic equality as a necessary, primary condition. Moreover, it is important that the methods of achieving this broader equality also have to be democratic in character. A system that uses coercive methods to achieve economic equality, for example, will not lead to a politically democratic system. The realization of this larger sense of equality can come only through understanding democracy as a state of life and not a state of politics alone. This sentiment is most forcefully voiced by Ambedkar when he writes:

> Some equate Democracy with equality and liberty. Equality and liberty are no doubt the deepest concern of Democracy. But the more important question is what sustains equality and liberty? Some would say that it is the law of the state which sustains equality and liberty. This is not a true answer. What sustains equality and liberty is fellow-feeling. What the French Revolutionists called fraternity. The word fraternity is not an adequate

---

11 Chandhoke and Kumar, 'Indian Democracy', p. 49.

expression. The proper term is what the Buddha called, Maitree. Without fraternity, liberty would destroy equality and equality would destroy liberty. If in Democracy liberty does not destroy equality and equality does not destroy liberty, it is because at the basis of both there is fraternity. Fraternity is therefore the root of Democracy.[12]

Principles of equality are not enough, even if they are sustained by law. Ambedkar rightly recognizes an inherent tension between liberty and equality, with the potential of each destroying the other. This is most powerfully captured in contemporary public discourse on merit versus reservation and on subsidies to the poor. In both these cases, the arguments refer back to the loss of one's liberty in a world of equality or the loss of equality in the primacy of liberty. Ambedkar's emphasis on fraternity as a necessary path to balance the contrary tensions in liberty and equality is important. His use of the phrase 'fellow-feeling' is suggestive that this is firstly a 'feeling', an experience. When equality is 'felt' along with institutional support, only then is there a possibility of democracy. The reason why 'feeling' is required is because the experience of equality is itself a problem. There is a sense of dispersion in this experience as there are conditions where, and under which, one is equal but conditions where one is not. The daily life and daily transactions of the people do not exhibit a constant sense and experience of equality. On the contrary, there are powerful experiences of inequality, such as those that lead to feelings of shame and humiliation. This is similar to the inability to experience justice in a way that injustice is often felt and experienced.

Thus, the notion of equality, when seen outside this experiential space, has to be produced and narrativized. It has to be

---

12 Ambedkar, 'Riddles in Hinduism', p. 283.

discovered and articulated. Social life is filled with examples of unequal access, unequal treatment, unequal behaviour. There is inequality in the roles people play in every transaction. In a bank, the customer is not equal to the manager in any sense of the word. In a shop, there is an obvious inequality between the shop owner and the customer. But in both these examples, one can still aspire to be treated equally. So the experience of inequality itself is only that which is legible in the background of another inequality. For example, if the bank manager treats me differently from another customer, then I feel that I am not being treated equally. But even as I can experience this inequality, it is only in the background of the unequal relationship between the manager and me. Thus, the experience of fellow-feeling in conjunction with the articulation of equality truly produces an experience of democracy and produces the social life of democracy.

Here is where protective discrimination or reservation policies are so essential, since expressions of equality without promoting a sense of fraternity are not useful. And how can one have a sense of 'fellow-feeling' if society is rigidly compartmentalized? How can one have fellow-feeling of any kind with people who are not allowed to enter spaces of mainstream society even though they constitute the majority of the society? Chandhoke and Kumar recognize this crucial element of Indian democracy when they note that 'protective discrimination policies are a second step towards realization of substantive equality', where the first step is the 'right to primary goods on non-market principles'.[13] Reservation policies have rightly been called one of the most important principles behind the success of Indian democracy. One can understand the necessity of it today when

---

13 Chandhoke and Kumar, 'Indian Democracy', p. 52.

we realize that the myth of 'We, the People' is sustained by the presence of a huge invisible population. These people, hundreds of millions in number, are invisible to mainstream society which has taken over the stakes in, and articulation of, democracy. Making these invisible people socially visible should be the first step in any action that can be called democratic. Once they are visibilized, then policies towards equality and social engineering leading to the possibility of fellow-feeling are the only ways by which we can truly aspire to be called a democratic nation. Reservation policies are one attempt towards this visibilization which, in the case of India, is the necessary precondition for any idea of democracy. I would go to the extent of saying that it is only reservation that has been the true success of Indian democracy so far; elections have been compromised long ago.

The problem of invisibility in Indian democracy is also related to an ethical question of who can represent whom in our society. In general, the common democratic norm is that anybody can stand for an election and, if elected, can perform the role of representing that constituency. While there are rules on who can stand for election, there is a deeper ethical problem at its core, and this has led to some unique qualities of Indian democracy. The question of who can represent whom has become quite central in discourses around identity. In the social sciences, Gopal Guru's critique about non-dalits representing dalits was connected deeply to the authority to do theory. His description of this situation as 'empirical shudras and theoretical brahmins' was critical of the view that certain types of people do not have the capacity to represent themselves and needed others to speak for them.[14] In theatre, this question was raised

---

14 For an extended debate on this issue, see Gopal Guru and Sundar Sarukkai, *The Cracked Mirror: An Indian Debate on Experience and Theory* (Delhi: Oxford University Press, 2012).

when white actors used to portray Black characters or men played roles of women, as was prevalent in earlier times. In literature, this question has spread its tentacles wide enough to question the legitimacy of those who write about communities to which they do not belong.

Representative democracy is an example of choosing somebody to speak on one's behalf. Since this is accomplished by members of the community through their choice in secret ballot, the ethical issues in this act have not been as prominent as other issues. The easiest way to deal with the ethics of who can speak for whom is solved in elections by electing people who belong to the social world of the voter. So, in India voting is very much dependent on caste identities, and candidates in every election are chosen keeping this in mind. To a somewhat lesser extent, so also with religious identities. However, this question of representation seems to arise only in the choice of the candidates before elections. The simple fact is that the representatives are far removed from the world of the common voter. They are displaced from them in so many different ways that they use their identity only as a means to enter the field. But the significant ethical question about representation has to be raised after the election. These are special challenges to Indian democracy given the many types of identities that have been created within the nation. Moreover, as Gopal Guru points out, the promise of liberal democracy in India has not really fructified for the dalits. He notes that 'a Dalit audit of liberal democracy over the past 60 years suggests that liberal democracy has proffered a skewed response to the Dalit question, one hinging on everyday forms of humiliation, degradation, and repulsion.'[15] He further argues

---

15 Gopal Guru, 'Liberal Democracy in India and the Dalit Critique,' *Social Research* 78(1) (2011): 99–122; here, p. 104.

that a very large segment of the dalits have remained invisible in this democracy and thus dalits 'from different segments have sought to critique liberal democracy for its failure to ensure substantive change with a sense of self-esteem and self-respect.'[16]

No idea of democracy can be divorced from the cultural baggage of the people in it, for after all democracy cannot be dissociated in any sense from the notion of 'the People'. And if some ideals of democracy are not part of the worldview of those cultures, then it is important to find ways to question, critique and modify those worldviews. Merely imposing democracy as a political system does not succeed in changing certain cultural practices by itself—this is precisely the point that Ambedkar makes in his critique of democracy as a purely governmental idea. And for any system that aspires to be democratic, even the changes in cultural values has to be done democratically. This is the greatest challenge to democracy: democracy cannot merely be a goal; the means towards that goal also has to be consistently democratic. Thus, the ethics of democracy is very closely related to the ethics of means and ends. In the global discourse, we can see that even as dominant Western democratic countries claimed to uphold values of democracy, in practice they were not democratic in their international relations or in positioning themselves in the world order.

Thus, the experience of democracy in India raises new theoretical possibilities and conceptual vocabularies which are necessary for understanding global democracy. There are many reasons why India's work on democracy is ignored, including an inherent colonial mindset of the major Western democratic powers. It is also a sad reflection on the labour of global scholarship and the way scholars have tended to understand the poor

---

16 Guru, 'Liberal Democracy in India', p. 117.

and the excluded. By ignoring most of the non-West and their unique experiments in democracy, international scholarship (primarily composed of a few dominant academic communities) has behaved in an extremely undemocratic manner. Talking about democracy is only performative if there is no social life to their ideas of democracy. It is not just the social or the economic elite that we need to consider but also the global intellectual elite who have become self-appointed interpreters of democracy and who have contributed to the alienation that has driven undemocratic politics, including the rise of the Right.

Instead of comparing with some model of democracy and judging Indian democracy based on those parameters, it is more important for the global community to understand the nature of Indian democracy and see whether there are any lessons that can be drawn from it. This argument also arises in the context of Europe confronting new challenges owing to migration and when notions of multiculturalism are bandied about in the West. Interestingly, Partha Chatterjee, in a new book titled *I Am the People*, shows how elements of Asian and African democracies are now being looked at by liberal democracies for their potential applicability in their own societies.[17]

The Chinese Model of Democracy

In December 2021, China's State Council Information Office released a white paper titled 'China: Democracy That Works.'[18] This document can be seen as an attempt to make a fresh assertion

---

17 Partha Chatterjee, *I Am the People: Reflections on Popular Sovereignty Today* (New York: Columbia University Press, 2020).

18 China State Council Information Office, 'China: Democracy That Works', *XinhuaNet*, 4 December 2021. Available at: https://bit.ly/3RyRWFl (last accessed on 12 July 2022).

about the democratic nature of the Chinese state against it being labelled otherwise. This note begins by pointing out that 'over the past hundred years, the Party has led the people in realizing people's democracy in China.' The fact that just one party rules the country could be seen as going against the basic tenets of democracy. However, the explanation in the paper demands a more careful analysis since it goes to the root of what democracy can and could mean. 'One party' is not seen as a problem since the document asserts that 'the People's status as masters of the country is the essence of people's democracy'. One-party rule can be contrasted with the dominantly two-party rule in the United States. If the number of parties alone is an indication of democracy, then the US and other Western democracies would pale in front of the multiplicity of political parties in India and many other non-Western countries.

In this document, a people's democracy is clearly defined in terms of its goals thus: 'Whole-process people's democracy integrates process-oriented democracy with results-oriented democracy, procedural democracy with substantive democracy, direct democracy with indirect democracy, and people's democracy with the will of the State. It is a model of socialist democracy that covers all aspects of the democratic process and all sectors of society. It is a true democracy that works.'[19] This definition does a great job of defining socialist democracy as a mix of many other forms of democracy!

The classification of different types of democracy signals the possibility of using democracy as a term to capture a variety of political actions. In each of these types, what is chosen to capture the essence of democracy are terms like 'whole-process', 'results-oriented', 'procedural', 'substantive', 'direct', 'indirect' and so

---

19 China State Council, 'China: Democracy That Works', p. 1.

on. In each of these types, the processes can be quite different and the mechanisms by which democracy functions can also greatly vary. The document offers a succinct definition of how a system should be evaluated as being democratic or not:

> The best way to evaluate whether a country's political system is democratic and efficient is to observe whether the succession of its leaders is orderly and in line with the law, whether all the people can manage state and social affairs and economic and cultural undertakings in conformity with legal provisions, whether the public can express their requirements without hindrance, whether all sectors can efficiently participate in the country's political affairs, whether national decision-making can be conducted in a rational and democratic way, whether people of high caliber in all fields can be part of the national leadership and administrative systems through fair competition, whether the governing party is in charge of state affairs in accordance with the Constitution and the law, and whether the exercise of power can be kept under effective restraint and supervision.[20]

The key points in this definition of democracy are about the rule of law and correctly following social and political order. This could be called 'legal democracy' in that the functions of what is called democratic are completely subsumed under law and legality. Here the notion of accountability of the leaders to the masses is built in. If accountability is indeed one of the core pillars of democracy, then is it possible to have a democratic system that has strong accountability but low individual choice? This takes us back to an age-old question of the slave and the master: If a master is good for the slave and keeps the slave

---

20 China State Council, 'China: Democracy That Works', p. 2.

comfortable, is there anything wrong about the system? What if a slave wants to be a slave of his or her own choice under a benign master? These questions are not merely academic points for discussion, since elected and unelected governments often use the same logic. If the goal of governance is the betterment of life for the citizens, then should it matter how the governing leaders are chosen? And if the citizens are happy with what a government does for them, then does it matter what form the government takes? Rather than dismissing these claims as anti-democratic, it is necessary to first engage with these arguments.

Democracies are strongly dependent on the rule of law since it is law that can institutionalize democratic ideals. However, having a purely law-driven system is not enough to call a country a democracy unless there is scope to challenge these laws, and processes to form new laws that are to the benefit of the people. This possibility is what makes legally driven social systems democracies. For example, autocratic societies can also function under the dictates of law—in fact, it is through draconian laws that such systems flourish. Democracy lies in the people's capacity to challenge these laws. In democratic countries, when such laws are passed most often in the name of 'national security' with no possibility of challenging them or having no mechanisms to control the abuse of such laws, they tend towards the autocratic system. A democratic system should allow for legitimate ways to challenge law and legality. Thus, there is enormous significance given to protests and dissent as embodying essential elements of democracy.

The Chinese document goes on to point out the function of democracy, and in the light of that description, we can ask whether dissent and protests do the job required of democracy. For a people's democracy as in the Chinese description, it is the people who are at the centre of this process. However, how the role of the people should be understood here is quite different from liberal democratic models. The Chinese argument about the primacy of the people is expressed as follows:

> Whether a country is democratic depends on whether its people are truly the masters of the country; whether the people have the right to vote, and more importantly, the right to participate extensively; whether they have been given verbal promises in elections, and more importantly, how many of these promises are fulfilled after elections; whether there are set political procedures and rules in state systems and laws, and more importantly, whether these systems and laws are truly enforced; whether the rules and procedures for the exercise of power are democratic, and more importantly, whether the exercise of power is genuinely subject to public scrutiny and checks.[21]

It is important to note the clear definition of what the goals of democracy are: there is absolutely no mention of contentious terms such as 'freedom of expression', 'freedom to dissent', etc. Although there is a mention of 'right to vote', it is unclear as to what kind of issues the people could vote on. Given that China is a one-party state, can people vote for candidates who are not in this monolithic party? The document points out that there is indeed an election because there are eight different political parties (but they all work under the Communist Party of China). It is also significant that the document explicitly suggests that the 'right to vote' is *less important* than the 'right to participate extensively'. It is clear that the vision of democracy here is more about involving as many people as possible. Voting, one might argue, aims to do this but does so quite imperfectly. Today,

---

21 China State Council, 'China: Democracy That Works', p. 2.

democracy has been reduced to a ritual of voting. Moreover, the numbers who vote in many democratic societies are many times fewer than half the eligible voters, and a democracy based on this form of voting alone as an imperfect form of people's participation. In the descriptions of democracy in the Chinese document, there is also a careful absence of the word 'choice'— a term that underlies many of the assumptions of liberal democracies. Thus, having only one dominant party—while it seems to go against the idea of choice—seems extremely reasonable when democracy is looked at from the perspective of the impact on people's lives rather than their right to make voting choices.

Well aware that China has been criticized for being anti-democratic—and this has increased since the post-2020 Hong Kong crackdowns—it is not a surprise to discover in this document the claim that democracy is not a universal term that can be judged by other countries. In a logic that has some problems, the document notes that '[w]hether a country is democratic should be judged by its people, not dictated by a handful of outsiders'.[22] The reason behind this argument is that there is no one model of democracy that every country has to follow as democracy 'manifests itself in many forms'. Moreover, echoing a point that is found across many Asian countries leading to the coinage of the term 'Asian democracy', this document too highlights the relation between the nature of democracy and culture. Thus, they claim that democracy is 'rooted in history, culture and tradition' and has different forms 'chosen by different peoples based on their exploration and innovation'.

Most interestingly, the document takes on a common criticism of democracy in China by combining the ideas of democracy and dictatorship as symbiotic elements of Chinese democracy:

---

22 China State Council, 'China: Democracy That Works', p. 2.

The Constitution describes China as a socialist country governed by a people's democratic dictatorship that is led by the working class and based on an alliance of workers and peasants. The fundamental nature of the state is defined by the people's democratic dictatorship. China upholds the unity of democracy and dictatorship to ensure the people's status as masters of the country. On the one hand, all power of the state belongs to the people to ensure that they administer state affairs and manage economic and cultural undertakings and social affairs through various channels and in various ways in accordance with the Constitution and laws; on the other hand, China takes resolute action against any attempt to subvert the country's political power or endanger public or state security, to uphold the dignity and order of law and safeguard the interests of the people and the state. Democracy and dictatorship appear to be a contradiction in terms, but together they ensure the people's status as masters of the country. A tiny minority is sanctioned in the interests of the great majority, and 'dictatorship' serves democracy.[23]

This explicit and bold assertion that democracy and dictatorship are not a contradiction is legitimized by the claim that such a process is the only way to maintain the role of 'the People' as 'masters of the country'. The document lists many schemes at the ground level that encourage people's participation in decisions related to governance. Their claim that such participation, which involves independent voting, is close to 90 per cent raises the level of democratic participation in China to a much greater degree than in countries like India, the US and other flag bearers

---

23 China State Council, 'China: Democracy That Works', pp. 9–10.

of democracy. Thus, this is a model of democracy which privileges democratic processes in smaller sectors rather than retain a notion of democracy only at the highest governing levels.

The weakness in reducing democracy to voting is explicitly criticized in the document. This articulation is also a stringent rebuke to the theatre of voting and elections in democratic systems.

> If the people are awakened only to cast a vote but become dormant afterwards, that is no true democracy. If the people are offered great hopes during electoral campaigning but have no say afterwards, that is no true democracy. If the people are offered fulsome promises during electoral canvassing but are left empty-handed afterwards, that is no true democracy. In China, the concept of democracy has taken root in the people's minds, and the practice of democracy has become an integral part of daily life and work, resulting in wide and sustained democratic participation. Democracy has become the norm, injecting great vitality into Chinese society.[24]

This argument will definitely be acceptable to all the models of democracy and there would be little dispute about the goals of this vision of democracy. It also marks a clear distinction between the macro picture of democratic governance and the micro conditions of democracy in daily lives that is integral to the success of macro governance. But like in every theory of democracy, the conceptually weak term here is 'people'. It is also a term that is most powerfully deployed. The statements above would be true if we understand clearly what is meant by 'the People'. Does it mean everybody in society? Every voting adult in society? There is the unsaid assumption that all the people

---

24 China State Council, 'China: Democracy That Works', p. 38.

collectively want something, want the 'same thing'. This is the crux of the problem in a democracy. 'People' as a term is collectively produced as if all the citizens are one unit called the people. In so doing, the aspirations and needs of this People are also seen to be homogenous and uniform. But in any society, this is rarely the case. There are different needs and different expectations from various groups within a society. The challenge in democracy is not to give everything everybody wants but to allocate resources based on various principles. And when people who don't get what they want protest, what does one do? The problem is that there is never one 'people' who have the same desires, visions and acceptance. The anti-democratic impulse comes originally from this desire for the oneness of all the people so that there is far greater control as well as greater efficiency in that control. But this is not the social reality. It is in engaging with the multiplicity of people and voices that the true function of democracy is really found. So while in principle the argument that more than the form of the government it is people's wishes that have to be respected makes perfect sense, in a diverse society this is just not possible since people's wishes may be diverse and sometimes contrary to each other. We have seen the troubling political response to expressions of diverse expectations within Chinese society. It is thus this concept of People that needs to be replaced with more nuanced notions so that in the name of the people, democratic impulses do not get destroyed.

But the point about locating the lifeworld of democracy within daily life and work is an important one and I would argue that such a view is an extension of Ambedkar's point about democracy and its relation to the larger society.

The Myth of 'the People'

Who is this People, this unified entity that is a darling of democracy? The popular definition of democracy taught right from schools—'Of the people, By the people, For the people'—clearly ties any idea of democracy to that of 'the People'. The Chinese use of the term 'people's democracy' and the way they define the goals of this democracy are also based on the primacy and value of this 'People'. Who really is it? Does such a concept exist? Does it have any reality in our societies? Does it refer to a singular entity, a homogenous set? Or is it a concept that is just put to rhetorical use? Is it a concept which, owing to its ambiguity, allows the true expectations of democracy to be glossed over? Is much of democracy about 'the People' only in name and not in any substantive sense?[25]

The relation between people and government reflects an ambiguity that is also present in the relation between the individual and society. It seems obvious that society is made up of individuals—but it is never a coherent collection of individuals. Even the idea of individuals when seen in relation to society is limited to the qualities of a person which can produce a coherent relationship with others. It is possible to have many individuals together in a room but if there is no meaningful relationship between them, then they do not form a group. Given a set of people, there are many conceivable relations between them.

---

25 For a critical discussion of the formation of 'We, the People' in the context of the Constituent Assembly debates, see Arvind Elangovan, ' "We the People?": Politics and the Conundrum of Framing a Constitution on the Eve of Decolonisation', in Udit Bhatia (ed.), *The Indian Constituent Assembly: Deliberations on Democracy* (London: Routledge, 2018), pp. 10–37. See also the analysis of 'people' in Dipesh Chakrabarty, ' "In the Name of Politics": Democracy and the Power of Multitude in India', *Economic and Political Weekly* 40(30) (23–29 July 2005): 3293–301.

There can be transactional relations such as between consumers and the owner of a grocery shop. There can be hierarchical relations such as in a classroom or in an office where employees report and answer to people at higher levels. There are some relations that can be classified as social. In spite of the ambiguity associated with the word, 'social' is a term we tend to not only use but also intuitively understand.[26] For instance, John Dewey's 'associated living' or Émile Durkheim's 'relation of association' or Ambedkar's notion of fraternity would qualify as interactions that can serve as the basis of a social relation. These relations are the glue that create a cohesive group among diverse individuals. The question is: What kind of a relation—or what kind of a social relation—is needed for a diverse set of individuals to coalesce into one group called 'the People'?

This question is fundamental to understanding the success and failure of democracies in different cultures. Like many in Asia claim, the idea of democracy in Asian countries has to be seen differently from that of the dominant West. However, it is important to specify in what sense they are different. One important difference is the nature of social relations—relations that bind individuals into a group. In many social phenomena including elections, emotions function as an essential binder. Conflicts arise when 'nation', which is largely understood as a legal category, gets converted by governments into an emotional relation. And it is precisely emotion as a category that eludes Western understanding of not just democracy but also the nature of individuals. Emotion has had a bad deal in Western intellectual thought, most powerfully illustrated in the assumed opposition between reason and emotion. In colonial discourses,

---

26 For a critical discussion of this concept, see Gopal Guru and Sundar Sarukkai, *Experience, Caste and the Everyday Social* (Delhi: Oxford University Press, 2019).

emotion has been identified with irrationality, with women and with Asians and Africans. The history of suspicion towards emotion is based on a selective reading of emotion as well as that of reason. It is the same concept of reason that Western Enlightenment (as exemplified in Kant, for instance) denied to Asian and African cultures, and to women in their own cultures. The derisive descriptions of Indians in colonial literature had much to do with the description of these people as emotional beings. Even the idea of theory, which attained the highest privilege in Western thought, was one that had to be carefully liberated from any association with emotion.

But democratic action is intrinsically associated with emotion. Dominant Western theories, cultivated on the bedrock of a suspicion of emotion, struggle to find the resources to handle emotion within their theories. Thus, when they are confronted with demagogues like Donald Trump, they are at a loss to make sense of it within their theoretical caves. The suspicion towards emotion is extended to experience as a category within the social sciences. Thus, the possibility that there can be other kinds of democracies follows very simply from the fact that the most basic concepts needed to define democracy—namely, individual, people, social, freedom, autonomy etc.—are terms that cannot be decoupled from the categories of emotion and experience, and thus have to be conceptualised differently. One way to deal with emotions, feeling and experience in democratic action is to reduce them to some form of reason. The only way that this can be done is if the individual is reduced to become part of the rational State. The rational citizen is given a choice to vote but the moment this is made explicitly emotional—as in every election in India or as in the case of Trump—then that becomes a crisis for these democracies.

Most liberal democracies built on this edifice are in a crisis because their value arises from the value of 'the People', but at the same time it is built on a view that is deeply suspicious of the possibility of a genuine collective called 'the People'. The suspicion that people can really come together is at the root of many of the institutional policies of Western democracies. In fact, the idea of 'one person, one vote' is as much a constraint on what an individual can do in a democracy and how much is allowed for an individual within this system. What really is the sacredness of 'one person, one vote'? While its value has been argued from a negative position that not all persons will be allowed to vote if this guarantee is not given, what is its value in itself? If everybody is allowed to vote, what does this singular association of a person with a vote actually entail? What greater significance does it have as far as the question of democracy is concerned?

When the idea of an individual is sanitized and reduced to quantitative measures, then there is no access to the kind of democracy that Ambedkar talks about or what some Asian democracies, with all their shortcomings, are pointing to. One consequence of this critique is to rethink the unit of democracy. The latest Oxfam report says that 98 families in India own the same amount of wealth as 522 million people.[27] Let us take the 98 families as being equal to 1,000 individuals. So 1,000 people own the same wealth as 522 million people! There is obviously something wrong with this ratio and it is not just in the inequality in society. It is also in the concept of the individual and the social that characterizes our society. When everything in society is so unequal and stands so much against 'one person, one house', or 'one person, one wealth', then why should this principle of 'one

---

27 Oxfam India, 'Inequality Kills: India Supplement 2022', 17 January 2022. Available at: https://bit.ly/3uLr9fc (last accessed on 12 July 2022).

person, one vote' have such a value? On the contrary, this 'one person, one vote' principle succeeds in hiding the inequalities in society and so simulates a value to democracy that is not sustainable as far as daily life in our societies is concerned.

In the political realm in which democracy is most invoked, the question of citizenship is converted to the right to vote. Voting is an expression of the 'will' of 'the People'. But not all can vote. Not even all citizens can vote. Young people below 18 cannot vote in India and in most other countries even though they are citizens of the country. Till a few decades back, women were not allowed to vote in many countries and today in many places prisoners are not allowed to vote. There are millions of others who cannot vote for one reason or other, some of which are deliberate, systemic attempts to keep people out of voting. The debate around the controversial Citizenship (Amendment) Act introduced by the BJP government in India in 2019 revolves around these issues. So the category of 'people' is not a simple collection of individuals; it is a term that is produced through political and moral categories.

The second problem is the expression of the 'will' of these people. This expression is often conflated with terms like autonomy, freedom, equality and so on. Like democracy, these terms too take different meanings in different contexts. Following the argument that I am making here about the idea of democracy being very closely tied to ideas of the individual and the social, so too are these terms. Firstly, an individual's action is often seen as an expression of an individual's will. How then does it become a collective will? Do all people 'will' something—together and at the same time? Or is it that there is only the will of a small group of powerful people that gets legitimized as the will of all people? One expression of this confusing idea of the collective will is freedom. Freedom is an extremely important idea that has been the bedrock of modernity and also one of the foundational markers of democracy. It has become enshrined in phrases like 'freedom of expression', 'freedom to act', 'freedom to dissent' and so on. But what does this concept actually mean? What is the relationship between freedom and the notions of self and the social, between the I and 'We, the People'? In the final part of the book, I explore this concept of freedom within democracy in greater detail.

The troubling truth about democracy is that even as it seems to promote and enhance the value of a free individual, the logic of democracy is operational only when the individual is subsumed and seen as part of 'the People'. There is a very interesting dialectic operating here: democracy attains value because it is seen as the expression of the 'will of the People', but the representatives of a democratic system act in ways that constantly attempt to convert the power of the 'we' to the privilege of the 'I'. The only way to recapture some meaningful sense of the individual as well as the collective is to recognize specific ethical foundations of democracy. In a later section, I discuss a few possible manifestations of the ethical imperative associated with the formation of the category of 'People' as well as the expression of the 'will of the People'.

Democracy as a form of social life challenges this myth of the people. If we want to take seriously Ambedkar's view of democracy, then it is necessary to reflect on how a society can be made democratic and not be content with a government that is only supposedly democratic. What is it to imagine a democratic society and not just a democratic government? How does a society become democratic? What are the obstacles to making a society democratic? It is not easy being democratic. It is easier to have a democratic government! The difficulty of living democratically can be experienced in our everyday life and it is necessary to understand these challenges in different domains of human action.

3.

DOMAINS OF DEMOCRACY

The life of democracy is one that has to be lived in the everyday and be manifest in all social actions. The reduction of the social life of democracy to the political is a way of ignoring this fundamental principle and a democracy cannot function effectively if this happens. It is a constant struggle to act in ways that are democratic, whether it be within families or in the social world. We have seen the phenomenon of political parties in India which suffer from a crisis of internal democracy, where power is often wielded by family members. Leaders are not chosen through transparent processes and often there is no space even for disagreements with them. How can we expect a party to govern a country democratically when there is such a lack of democracy within the organization itself?

For, after all, to learn to be democratic is to first practise it in our own daily lives. We are often confronted by the difficulty of being democratic in our engagement with our families, friends, peers and in public space. The moment individuals decide not to be democratic in their personal actions, it becomes easier to not be democratic in the public and political space. Thus, democracy can only be a matter of habit, a matter of personal and social practice across all domains. In this sense, democracy is a way of life, the way we perform all our actions. It is a deep engagement with the way we understand ourselves in relation to others.

So what is it to be democratic in everyday life? Family is a good starting point, especially in the context of non-Western societies where the influence of the family is paramount. Much of the idea of the social is first formed within the dynamics of the family. Family as a social unit across Asia and Africa is quite distinct from the way the family functions in many Western societies. But what is it to be democratic in a family? While there are various forms of power dynamics within a family depending on whether it is 'traditional' or 'modern', we can look at one simple and undisputable function of asymmetry between parents and their children. Within the family, the parents take some decisions with or without discussion with all members of the family. There are some decisions in which the children will perforce not be part. In such a case, one cannot claim that the family is an undemocratic space based on the assumption that democracy means to have equal say in all matters. The dynamics of the particular type of decision will necessarily reduce it to a decision that can be made only by the parents. When this 'freedom' to exercise judgement on behalf of children is extended to all actions concerning the children, the children will begin to see it as an undemocratic household. Within these practices, they learn that certain kinds of actions are exclusive. It is not surprising then that even democratic governments repeatedly use this image of the family: from wanting to be seen like a benign patriarch to denying citizens access to certain sectors of governance in the name of security. A government that looks upon its citizens as children cannot really be a democratic government. And this is an attitude that is first cultivated within the family.

To understand the functioning of democracy, we can begin with the family as the model. Rather than asking whether a family is democratic based on the definition of political democracy, we can ask what could a democratic space within a family look like. The first obvious difference between a government and a family is that there is no choice in the creation of a family unlike that of a government through a democratic election. We do not elect our parents or siblings. In the case of the family, democracy is not a process that leads to the institution that governs the family. However, this does not mean that the process of governing the family is outside the ambit of democratic action. The immediate criticism of this claim would be that a family is not a space in which democratic actions are applicable. But this is precisely the point. Governments tend to use this assumption when they describe their society or nation as a family. Calling the nation a family allows the practices within a family to be taken into the orbit of politics, and through this, undemocratic and patriarchal practices become part of governance.

To articulate the possibility of democracy within a family, we have to rethink many of the assumptions that are accepted as norms in a family. Take, first, the wealth held by the family. Let us assume, as is generally the case, that the wealth in a family is the money earned by the parents. If so, then who does this wealth belong to? To each of the parents or to the family as a whole? The first challenge to the idea of democracy within a family rests on this question. If the wealth is seen to belong to the entire family as such, then the next question is: who has a say in how it is used? Should the parents discuss with their children how money is spent? An immediate answer would be that the children are not competent to know how to spend money and thus there is no need for the adults to consult them. Instead, the parents would argue that they spend for the well-being of their children. This argument parallels that of the government's response regarding the governance of wealth that belongs to all its citizens. People as a category become like children. The government acts for the well-being of the people like parents act for the well-being of their children. The government will not discuss everything with the people since the people, like children, do not have the competence to discuss 'adult' matters like economic policies, foreign policies, national security and so on. Thus, the creation of a 'specialist elite' which will mediate between the people and the government. Interestingly, in the case of the family, schools and teachers begin to function like the specialist elite in that they produce the necessary competence in children to become decision-making adults.

So the first step is to question whether the family wealth completely 'belongs' to the adults in the family. Or if this sounds too 'radical', we could rephrase this by asking what does 'belong' mean. What can somebody do with the money that 'belongs' to them? By the very definition of the family, the wealth should belong equally to all and the adults can only act as trustees of the wealth even though they are the ones earning it. Otherwise, the notion of a family itself is called into question, since the family is the first and the most robust example of a group of individuals who are bound together through relations of fraternity. To argue that a family is different from social groupings is to understand the social in a restricted manner. Instead, the family should be seen as the domain where the first experiences of relating to others and the first experience of the social are formed.[1] Thus, democratic action within the family introduces a sense of trusteeship, a term that, as we will see later, has a deep connection to

---

1 See Gopal Guru and Sundar Sarukkai, *Experience, Caste and the Everyday Social* (Delhi: Oxford University Press, 2019).

democracy. The parents truly are the trustees of their children, but being trustees is not the same as having the freedom to do whatever one wants.

Justifying an action by saying that it is for the well-being of the children is in principle a nondemocratic action since this argument has been used to justify all kinds of impositions on children and as an extension, people. It is an essential ingredient of all hierarchies including those of gender, class and caste. At the same time, it is also true that children may not be the best judge of how to spend money in the best interests of the family. So how does one reconcile this tension in incorporating the views of the children for a 'democratic'—that is, inclusive—decision about all matters related to the family? Even though one could argue that children are too young to take meaningful decisions, there are many decisions taken within a family in which a democratic process is possible. For example, if one of the parents has to change their job and move to another city, a discussion on all the aspects of this move with the children may be all that is required. In other words, while the decision may be taken by a few, the participation of all seems to be a necessary condition for an act to be seen as democratic. The strength of a democracy is the strength of the participation of all who are involved in the definition of the group—whether it is a family, an institution, a caste group or the nation. The practice of democracy within families is the first step in the establishment of democracy as a way of life. In societies in which the sense of family is extended to people other than the parents, children learn very important lessons about social relations, including that of democratic relations. The characteristics of democratic behaviour that can arise in families include trusteeship, trusting others who are not as 'old and wise' as the elders, who are not as educationally and technically qualified as the parents, who do not have any expert knowledge yet should be included and involved in actions that impact all the members of a family.

We can extend this to other domains in which we learn the practice and meaning of democracy. The first domain outside the family which a child ideally encounters is the school. (It is important to remember here that millions of children do not have this luxury of going to school and instead enter informal and exploitative work environments. Obviously, for them democracy is not even an imagined ideal in the contexts in which they live and work.) For these children, educational institutions in general become the space for understanding democracy as a process of life. How does democracy function within schools? Typically, in schools, parents are replaced by teachers, although teachers differ from parents in various ways. However, the sense of care and dedication to improving the children's skills for their 'own good' brings parents and teachers into a common space. Yet there is a sense of depersonalization in the classrooms. For the students, moving away from the personal means looking at the adults—the teachers—differently. They cannot take certain liberties with the teachers as they can do with their parents or their extended family. But here too, as far as the syllabus, pedagogy, evaluation and other aspects of school education are concerned, there is little inclusivity, trusteeship and participation. In such a scenario, generally in large public schools, the space for democratic action is very limited. (Elite private schools in India often distinguish themselves from these public schools by pointing to processes of inclusivity and participation, but how democratic they really are is open to debate.) Here the challenge to democracy comes from a slightly different impulse than within families. Schools produce the first experiences of a larger social where children cohabit in a common space with other children whom they might never meet as part of familial interactions. What kind of experiences can they learn from the school? They learn about competition, hierarchies based on skills and examination results, about differentials of behaviour among one another and with the teachers, about the many inequalities manifested in clothes, food, travel and so on. In India today, there is little in the general school experience that teaches children how to be democratic and what it is to be democratic.

Hence, the first step is to visualize what a life of democracy in schools could be like. Some of these principles are recognized as part of the best practices of teaching, but they have to be reoriented as practices of democracy and not of just learning per se. For example, not talking down to the children, letting them understand the content of the text from their own perspectives, listening to their responses to what they learn, teaching them to disagree with what is being taught, and encouraging them to listen to their peers and learn from one another—these are all practices that work towards creating a life of democracy. Some of these may be practised in some schools. But if they are taught as part of the strategies of teaching or if they are seen as skills related to knowing and knowledge, they would not lead to a social life of democracy. It is only when these principles become life practices that children learn the experience of democracy which they can deploy in the larger society, including in politics.

Similarly, institutions offer other important lessons for the success and failure of democracy. Today there are very few institutions in India that are truly democratic. Take the domain of private companies and private institutions in general. The value attached to certain notions of the private has allowed the private to escape most of the requirements of democratic action even when situated within a democratic society. And this is the ultimate tragedy—since most societies have moved towards private ownership. The impact of this shift is most starkly visible in the accumulation of global wealth in the hands of a very few individuals, all of them associated with private enterprises. And politicians in both democratic and authoritarian systems have also amassed untold wealth and have, for all purposes, become representatives of the private while being in a position of governing the public.

Indian institutions are particularly undemocratic in the way they function, as the hierarchies within families and society get absorbed into institutions. One would think that perhaps academic institutions would be different, given that they teach and write so much on aspects like freedom and democracy. But they are also notoriously undemocratic in their functioning. While there may be processes within public universities and well-funded science institutions, the culture of governance does not exhibit the kind of freedoms that a democracy is supposed to have. Students hardly have a voice, faculty in most cases cannot easily act as a collective, many decisions of the administration are not public and accountable—the list goes on and on. In many private academic institutions, even faculty meetings are rarely held and there are no open processes and discussions on hiring and other policies. If this is the case with educational and research institutions, one can imagine how much worse it is in other private institutions. Even public government offices are infamously secretive; the resistance to the successful implementation of the Right to Information Act, one of the most important steps to transparency in government, is an indication of the challenges of developing a culture of democracy in India. The pervasive lack of democracy in the day-to-day functioning of these offices is reflected in the lack of democratic practices in political governance. How is it possible to have democratic politics if there is such a lack of democracy at every stage of our lives and at every level in our society? At each of these stages and levels, certain core qualities of democracy are absent. And these are the very people, coming from these families, schools and institutions, who become politicians and hence part of the political system.

Thus, it is reasonable to suggest that the first condition for the production and sustenance of democracy in a society, in the vision of Ambedkar, is the production of a democratic self. The demand that each of the domains of social action (the family, the school, the professional and political institutions, and so on) follow democratic practices can be made only if the self of the individual acting in each of these domains is democratic—a state that I refer to as a democratic self. It is the qualities of the self that we need to focus upon. While this might seem to reduce democracy to certain dispositions of individuals, it is not necessarily the case since much depends on how the individual is defined. Western democracies arise in cultures where there is a privileging of individuals as autonomous monads. What about the notion of the individual in societies where such a possibility is not present? What are the implications of defining the individual and the social in a completely different manner? It is irrational to expect that democratic practices based on an autonomous and independent individual (exemplified in the 'one person, one vote' principle) will also be equally applicable to societies in which an individual is defined in a far more complex manner. When people are surprised that voting in India is done based on group memberships or that politicians do not seem capable of being independent of their families, it is not just a matter of corruption or selfishness. It also embodies a struggle with understanding what autonomous individual action can be in their societies.

A Democratic Self

If we invoke the idea of a self—that which defines what individuals are, which allows us to form beliefs about each of ourselves— then does that go against the fundamental idea of democracy as something to do with others, groups and people as a whole? I concluded the last section by pointing out that the cultivation of a democratic self is the first condition for producing and sustaining a democratic society. This shift is the foundation for the creation of a democratic government. What this means is that to be democratic we have to first inquire how each of us can be democratic in our relations with parents, children, family members, strangers, colleagues and others.

The production of a democratic self is the way a social life of democracy is produced. To recognize that this idea is not a fancy dream, think of the enormous effort put into making individuals into reasoning selves. Modernity is characterized by repeated calls for individuals to take on the burden of reason and to train themselves to reason for themselves. But to produce this reasoning self, not only does society promote ideas of reason but it enforces it through education. The teaching of disciplines like mathematics and science to all children from the very beginning is one way of enforcing specific ways of reasoning. Thus, the question is not whether it is meaningful to produce democratic selves but, rather, how this could be done.

The concern with the self is also a very special concern for cultures in the Global South. And the selves in operation in these cultures are never independent individual selves, like in dominant cultures of the West, but always a social self. The emphasis on individual autonomy at the expense of family and community is not traditionally found here. And even in contemporary times, there is a constant struggle between the individual autonomous self and the social self of individuals.

I will begin by making a simple point: the notion of an individual autonomous self is itself a type of social self. It is a product of particular forms of society which create value for such an idea. Such an individual self is valorized because of the social value it acquires, not just from the intellectual class but also from commercial interests. It is not a surprise that the most common expression of individual autonomy in many of our societies is through the notion of consumerist choice. In fact, the production of the individual as a unique and privileged concept that characterizes modern Western societies is only possible by various processes. An important one among them is the postulation of the mind as distinct from the body, and placing the capacity for reason primarily within that of the mind. This dualism between body and mind, most famously associated with Descartes, also leads to the growth of 'rationalism' as a doctrine. The Cartesian mind is not just separated from the body, it is also separated from society, from others. This artificial exclusion of the body, as well as the social from the individual mind, reaches its crescendo in the slogans of modernity. However, it is also a point that is being increasingly challenged today.

There is a growing argument, drawing from work in different disciplines such as cognitive science, biology and philosophy, that the independence of the individual mind and society is not to be taken at face value. If we consider mind as something to do with 'mental states' such as belief, dispositions, emotions and thinking, then it is not possible to hold naive beliefs about the independence of the individual mind from society. There have been different models of how we could view the social mind based on the fact that perception, sensory experiences and representations are all social in character, in that they are learned from others and are products of history and culture. One particularly powerful argument is that even if there is something like the individual mind, it is only a holder of all the social meanings as well as of rules about perception, emotion, representation and so on.[2] Such arguments are further supported by the presence of collective or group intelligence among many insects and animals, where these creatures think as a collective and not as independent, separate individuals. Humans too think collectively, sometimes in an obvious manner like in mobs and sometimes more implicitly. One of the powerful arguments for this view is that our cognitive states are deeply dependent on language and language itself is inherently social, having been produced socially. Such arguments have been made from different approaches: from Buddhist arguments about the self and meaning, non-dualistic arguments about the falsity of distinct selves, Karl Marx's observation that the 'cultivation of the five senses is the work of all previous history', and contemporary accounts such as Eviatar Zerubavel's argument for a 'sociology of thinking'.

These arguments support the primacy of a social self over the individual self. This also suggests therefore that the primacy given to the individual self is itself a product of social thinking at a particular time in the evolution of societies. Many social processes can be explained much better by the idea of a social self. The we-experience is one of the most important experiences that we have as a group and is similar to the I-experience in many ways. Identity is an expression of a we-self. This social self does all the work that the individual self does: we talk about experiences as if they are common to the group (such as caste experience and gender experience); a group has a collective memory just like individual memory; many times the collective self overrides the individual self when a person begins to function more

2 See Laurence Kaufmann, 'Social Minds' in Ian C. Jarvie and Jesus Zamora-Bonilla (eds), *The SAGE Handbook of the Philosophy of Social Sciences* (London: Sage, 2011), pp. 153–80.

as a member of a group; and the social self, like the narrative individual self, produces social narratives about a collective.[3]

There are two very important ideas of self in the Indian context that I believe would be essential to a discussion of a democratic self. One of the most powerful expressions of a democratic self comes through the idea of self-rule, an idea that was most important to Gandhi. And the other notion that is often counterposed to this is Ambedkar's notion of self-respect. Both these notions are specific formulations of the self and it is my contention that they are both expressions of a democratic self that is primarily social in character and that both of them lead to the possibility of a social life of democracy.

Gandhi's notion of self is fundamentally associated with his idea of swaraj. The word swaraj means self-governance, and at first reading it seems to be primarily about governing our individual self, controlling our actions and so on. But swaraj as a term has a wider meaning, and a particular idea of the social enters this notion of governing our selves. Gandhi calls for swaraj for the nation, but it is also swaraj for the individual, because without that it is impossible to attain freedom for the nation. Anthony J. Parel argues that there are four meanings of swaraj: national independence; political freedom of the individual; freedom from poverty; and an individual's capacity for self-rule (spiritual freedom).[4] In an insightful analysis of Gandhi's notion of swaraj and as a response to Parel, Nishikant Kolge and N. Sreekumar point out that these are not four independent notions; rather, they are all related to each other.[5] They argue

---

3 For more detailed discussion on these aspects, see Guru and Sarukkai, *Experience, Caste and the Everyday Social.*

4 Anthony J. Parel, 'Introduction: Gandhian Freedoms and Self-Rule' in Anthony J. Parel (ed.), *Gandhi, Freedom, and Self-Rule* (New York and Oxford: Lexington Books, 2000), pp. 1–24.

that for Gandhi, '[the] idea of swaraj or independence for the nation [. . .] is a collective capacity to live together in peace and harmony. He writes in *Hind Swaraj* that it is swaraj when we learn to rule ourselves and it is, therefore, in the palm of our hands'.[6] Gandhi's views on swaraj are actually a perfect fit for what we would mean by democracy today. Gandhi affirms that 'we cannot have swaraj until we have made ourselves fit for it', which is exactly what is needed for a sustainable social life of democracy. Moreover, Gandhi did not subscribe to the foundational suspicion towards individuals. His view, as the authors argue, was 'based on the assumption that man is not born to live in isolation but is essentially a social animal, independent and interdependent'.[7] There is no better expression of the centrality of the social self and its essential role in producing the social life of democracy.

The other significant contribution to the argument for a democratic self can be found in Ambedkar's concept of self-respect, a concept very important to him as expressed in his oft-quoted comments: 'It is disgraceful to live at the cost of one's self-respect. Self-respect is the most vital factor in life. Without it, man is a cipher.' And 'Nothing is more disgraceful for a brave man than to live life devoid of self-respect.' D. R. Nagaraj, in his seminal work *Flaming Feet*, presents the contrary positions of Gandhi and Ambedkar as a contrast respectively between self-purification and self-respect. However, although there is quite a bit of discussion on what self-purification could be, there is

---

5 Nishikant Kolge and N. Sreekumar, 'Towards a Comprehensive Understanding of Gandhi's Concept of Swaraj: Some Critical Thoughts on Parel's Reading of Swaraj' in Siby K. Joseph and Bharat Mahodaya (eds), *Reflections on Hind Swaraj* (Wardha: Institute of Gandhian Studies, 2010), pp. 171–93.

6 Kolge and Sreekumar, 'Towards a Comprehensive Understanding', p. 177.

7 Kolge and Sreekumar, 'Towards a Comprehensive Understanding', p. 180.

little about self-respect.[8] At one level, this concept seems self-evident and is merely an expression that one has to have some respect for oneself. But there is an important social context to this concept that has to be uncovered. The challenge of living with respect is always with respect to another, particularly another in whose eyes there is no respect for the individual. The person who lives with self-respect responds to the humiliations forced upon them by somebody in a socially superior hierarchical position. Self-respect arises as a way of accepting what one is to oneself and not to see oneself through the eyes of another, particularly those who denigrate the individual.

In this context, it is useful to consider Periyar's views on self-respect and, in general, the influence of this idea in the non-brahmin movement in Tamil Nadu. Periyar's invocation of self-respect was significant for its role in his fight against brahminism and untouchability. He made an important distinction between swaraj and self-respect, which led to his fissure with Gandhi. Unhappy that the swaraj movement was not able to acknowledge the necessity of the destruction of the varnashrama dharma (the system that legitimizes caste practices), he attacked the focus on swaraj in place of self-respect. He argued that 'Swaraj is possible only where there is already a measure of self-respect.' Periyar's arguments clearly illustrate that 'self-respect, as percept and practice, was to be considered a political and ethical counter to the ideal of self-rule.'[9]

---

8 For a discussion on self-esteem and self-respect in the context of liberal democracy, see Guru, 'Liberal Democracy in India', p. 104.

9 Quoted in V. Geetha and S. V. Rajadurai, *Towards a Non-Brahmin Millennium: From Iyothee Thass to Periyar* (Kolkata: Stree-Samya, 1998), pp. 285, 283. I thank Sayoni Ghosh for emphasizing this point and Srinivasan Ramanujam for discussions on Periyar.

As in the case of swaraj, we can identify different types of self-respect. There is self-respect of labour, of one's wealth, of one's social position, of one's occupation, among others. Self-respect becomes important for the oppressed classes because it is the mechanism through which respect from other members of the society is made possible. Furthermore, there is an explicit connection between democracy and respect. In fact, I would suggest that when self-rule and self-respect are seen through the conceptual prism of democracy, we can perceive the similarity between the concerns of Gandhi and Ambedkar. The interesting parallel between these two is as follows: to govern a society, what is first needed is the capacity for self-governance. So to govern democratically, what is needed is a democratic cultivation of the self, a democratic self. Just as governance is closely related to democracy, so too is respect. Democracy is deeply based on the notion of respect. The expressions that are often used to describe the democratic process include the following: 'respect people's wishes in an election', 'respect your opponent', 'respect the results of an election', 'respect the rules of democracy'. It is important to recognize that the word 'respect' is crucial to these expressions. For a democratic society, it would not be possible to replace 'respect' with 'follow', although the connotation of respect in the above expressions is not very different from 'follow'. Or even 'accept', like the statement 'accept the people's wishes' or 'accept the results of the election'. Neither 'accept' nor 'follow' capture the democratic ethos because both these words are passive. It tells people what to do without a deeper under-standing of what the processes of election or democracy are. But the term 'respect' puts the agency into the individual. In a demo-cratic society, the politician does not just 'follow' the people's wishes but respects them. We are not expected to just follow certain rules but to respect them. The corollary of this is that it is only after the process of cogitating and coming to respect something that we will decide to follow it. Thus, Ambedkar's and Periyar's comments about self-respect should be seen as fundamental to the practice of democracy, because to have respect among people in a society or respect for social processes, first there must be self-respect. The necessity of respect for fraternity—which, for Ambedkar, is the foundation of democracy—clearly links respect with democracy. Invoking the idea of self-respect then is to invoke the idea of a democratic self based on respecting itself, being in fraternity with oneself. This is a social self and supplies the contour of a social life of democracy.

Both self-governance and self-respect are fundamentally related to labour. A significant component of self-governance can be seen as self-labour and a crucial social meaning of self-respect revolves around respect for the labour one does. The relationship between caste and labour makes self-respect a most important ideal, as exemplified in Ambedkar. Thus, focussing on swaraj and self-respect actually leads to the recognition of the essential role that labour plays in the practice of democracy, particularly in the formation of the social life of democracy.

Labour

For whom does democracy really matter? How does democracy enter the daily lives of the people it is supposed to function on behalf of? Looking at people's indifference to governmental politics in everyday life, it might seem that democracy as a system is quite irrelevant to the people it is supposed to serve. Democracy comes to life during elections, like another festival day, but one that comes once in a few years, depending on what type of elections are held. Some may participate in this festival in earnest; others get paid for it or receive inducements to vote.

But the absence of a democratic culture in everyday life makes democracy an alien experience. Even in the act of voting, there is a minimal understanding of the larger functions of democracy. Why is democracy so invisible to the people? Even after politicians are voted to power, there is little about the processes and functions of democracy that is communicated to the people. People read about what a government does and does not do but in general these actions do not succeed in producing a coherent narrative of democracy. How is a narrative of democracy and how are the experiences of what it is to be democratic produced in a society? Interestingly, it is much easier to produce narratives and experiences of authoritarian rule and to communicate and transmit them. Teaching what it is to be democratic in a society that has not imbibed it in its daily life is not only a difficult task but also one that has serious implications for the functioning of such a society.

However, even though democracy is not explicitly present in everyday life, there is an implicit presence through which the ideas of democracy seep into the consciousness of a society. And this happens through labour. Labour does a double task: as an organizing principle of society, labour impedes the everyday consciousness of democracy but at the same time is necessary for the development of a democratic ethos. I would argue that labour is the most important among all concepts in its relation to democracy as it is also central to the formation of individual and social selves. The predominant experience of everyday life is labour, the constant work that we keep doing. Even leisure is an absence of work, and its commodification today has made leisure and entertainment a form of work.

What does it mean to say that labour impedes the engagement with democracy as a social value? The relationship between democracy and labour can be seen most starkly in the functions of everyday life. For a majority of people in our society, the day begins with work. Whether in villages or in urban areas, work organizes not just the time of the day but almost everything else, such as the place where one lives, where their children study and so on. Almost without exception, the workspace is undemocratic. In villages, where labourers work the fields, feudalism exists at different levels—from an openly and brutally repressive feudal lord to a more nuanced form in which workers are completely in the grip of employers. Millions who are self-employed, running small shops, hotels and such, are too busy surviving the various pressures of everyday life. The situation in cities and towns is not that different for the lower classes who have to struggle to make enough to survive in a difficult urban environment. This means that democracy as an idea or as praxis is not available to most people in a society. Since they have little time for it, democracy becomes a form of leisure that they cannot afford, leading the well-to-do classes (many of whom do not even vote) to become the public representatives of the supporters of democracy. The social structure of work also keeps the lower classes deprived of the benefits of being in a democratic society. Many times this alienation of the majority from political democracy appears as indifference. Most common people seem quite indifferent to who is 'ruling' the state or is in power at the centre. The centralized process of governance is alienating to their lives; at the most, democratic politics only enters their lives during elections to local bodies. The fundamental point is that the vast majority of the people simply do not have the time to engage with the idea of democracy. As long as notions of democracy do not enter their labour for survival, democracy is scarcely meaningful or important.

At the same time, the very possibility of labour depends on practices of social governance. The government, whether in the state or at the centre, influences labour, as its economic policies bring labour to the villages, through government and private-sector employment as well as support to domains such as agriculture. Although not explicitly articulated in the consciousness of everyday life, democracy arises through people's participation in labour that is influenced by government policies. How we think about labour and engage with it will deeply influence the production of a democratic self. In particular, the possibility of self-governance as well as self-respect, as two modes of producing a democratic self, are also linked to how labour is allowed to function in society. Thus, labour is one of the most powerful ways by which the individual self, the social self and democracy definitively come together in society.

The formation of the social self is deeply indebted to labour. In fact, it could be argued that it is labour that does the groundwork for the establishment of the caste system in India, which is both formed and legitimized through labour. The practices of caste that reduce and essentialize the many qualities of an individual to only the labour that she does are first and foremost anti-democratic acts—for in reducing an individual to one element of her existence, the shared commonality with others who labour differently is erased. Labour that is an individual human action is converted into a social term called caste. The fact that even today caste consciousness is still so dominantly understood in terms of labour shows the power of producing such a social self distinguished by labour. Even when members of these caste groups work in other professions, their association with their 'original' labour continues to play an important role in denying them respect. In emphasizing caste as a primary social term, what is lost is the importance of understanding the sociality of labour as well as the impact that notions of labour have on the formation of both individual and social selves.

Any idea of democracy is essentially linked to labour and the forms of labour in society. Alongside, there is also the labour of democracy itself—a particular form of labour—the work that needs to be done to be democratic. In the discussion of democratic practice in different domains, it is clear that what was at stake was the type of labour needed to make these domains democratic. And often, the confusion about the nature of democracy is compounded by the lack of a clear understanding of the labour associated with democracy. The act of voting and that of getting elected do not really constitute the labour of democracy. One of the biggest problems in the public acceptance of democracy is the cynicism towards the elected politician, which is also influenced by certain views about the nature of political work. The vast number of people with criminal records who are elected or the kind of 'goondas' who become representatives of the people, often makes the category of the politician a contested figure. Even movies often portray the brutal power of politicians who misuse their power over police and other agents of the administration, thereby creating the image of a democratic representative who is totally authoritarian. Thus, members of the middle and aspiring classes prefer not to let their children participate in politics, that is, to do the labour of politics. This reaction to the labour of politics is a major contributing factor to the role of families in politics. Due to this attitude, the work of politics too gets absorbed into the hereditary logic of caste.

Today, there are claims of democratic action through social media. Democracy has been reduced to voicing one's opinion on Facebook, Twitter, WhatsApp and so on. While this media does have mobilizing capabilities, its facile connection to democracy should be questioned. We can do this by first examining the nature of the labour of democracy. What work does social media do in the name of democracy? Whatever else be its impact, social media, consisting of individuals often hiding in anonymous shells, is by itself not conducive to the production of the social life of democracy.

Labour is also the concrete way by which the abstract notion of 'the People' becomes actualized in any society. Thus, we cannot have an ideal democracy without reformulating the question of labour. We can clearly see this in Gandhi, whose idea of democratic action was closely linked to challenges to certain hierarchical notions of work, such as the well-known example of cleaning toilets. It is through this emphasis on labour that we can try to understand not only the Chinese document on democracy discussed earlier but also, in general, the Asian cultural models of democracy. If the notions of equality and freedom cannot be dissociated from the idea of labour and how labour is organized and respected, then the true 'cultures of democracy' are in reality reflections of 'cultures of labour'. In India, given that the social structure of caste is itself based on certain notions of labour, it is understandable that any idea of democracy that is functional within such a society has to be reflective of these metaphysical foundations of labour. For example, much has been written about the labour of running a household. The invisibility of this labour and its non-recognition as meaningful economic work has led to a corrosive rejection of the role women, through the running of households, have in society. Alongside, there is the society composed of the domestic labouring class. A whole system of social practices is developed around the way this labour is treated. There is a system of networked governance between sometimes visible and many times invisible members of the public who decide on salaries, leave, loans etc. paid or given to this class, which mostly consists of women. The women who employ, control and govern domestic labour justify their practices as if they are part of systemic rules that apply to this sector.

This is one of the most undemocratic of spaces since many anti-democratic practices get legitimized here. Again, there are two points that should capture our attention here: the anti-democratic practices engendered in this domain often lead to lack of self-governance (swaraj of the individuals who depend on domestic labour) as well as lack of respect for the work these labourers do. This is not merely an economic problem but an example of the way democratic ethos in the social life influences responses in political democracy.

So how is it possible to make explicit the link between labour and democracy? I would see any project that does this as working towards producing a social life of democracy and towards realizing Ambedkar's contention that democracy is a form of society. The first democratic action is through participating in the labour of others. Today, equality is often bandied around as an individual right. Equality is not really substantive if it is reduced to an equality of entitlement. The expression 'we are all equal' has to have a counterpart in action: that is, all labour has to be valued equally. Obviously, this might sound absurd—since, for instance, a manager might have to do more work compared with a new entrant to a factory. But we are not talking about equality in terms of an equal-pay structure; rather, of equality in terms of social value. This equality of value of all labour is a necessary condition for the possibility of a democratic society, since for a society to exist, it essentially needs different labouring classes. Acknowledging that there will be differences in skill, in output and in economic worth, we can still demand the production of equal social value for all labour. One expression of this is respect for all professions. Unfortunately, the structures of all our societies are such that there is a completely skewed hierarchy of values of labour, with so-called menial labour being low on this scale. Scavenging labour is placed at the end of the list and it is not a surprise that those who perform this labour are viewed as if they are the very bottom of society. Equality in the context of democracy has to begin with articulating and establishing equality of the value of labour. In this sense, one can see that for Gandhi the insistence on individuals cleaning their toilets was part of this attempt to articulate democracy that is based on participative labour and not just participative politics. (I mention this example again because in the everyday life of the dominant castes, I most often find that the labour of cleaning one's own toilet is still seen as the most unclean act and one that has to be done by a particular labouring class. This lesson is most powerfully embedded in the minds of children from these families right from a very young age.) It is the reaction against labour that creates a non-democratic society, and it is a deeply flawed assumption that democracy can be produced without addressing this inequality and simply through political participation alone.

There are two aspects of non-democratic practice present in contemporary practices of labour. One is the set of labour practices that will not be performed by others in society. This is well exemplified by both the caste and the class system. The upper and middle castes will not perform the labour that the dalits are supposed to do. As the example of scavenging labour shows, it is the idea of labour that is so closely linked to the production of non-democratic thought in such a society. At the other end, there is labour which is outside the purview of the marginalized and the poor, not because of any fiat about their origins but because of their 'qualifications'. Although these qualifications are often presented as cognitive skills required for a job, they are in fact products of social structures and social prejudices. Qualifications and skills, particularly in the oft-repeated rhetoric of merit, are social concepts and not cognitive ones alone. The double whammy is this: the poor and the marginalized cannot get out of the labour they are caught in and so have to continue to do the work which the 'others' will not do; at the same time, they cannot access the labour that creates wealth for the aspiring classes owing to social rules that operate in the name of education and skills. My point is that since democracy is intrinsically associated with labour, social practices that cannot engage with labour in a greater spirit of fraternity become the biggest impediment to envisioning a truly democratic society. Any truth about democracy can only be discovered by re-examining its relationship with labour.

The two most powerful domains that form the background of democratic processes in contemporary society are science and technology, and religion. We live in a world that is dominated by the technological. We also find that religion is playing an ever-increasing role in global politics. In India, religion has always been integral to everyday life. Labour today is closely linked with science and technology. How do these two domains relate to democratic practices? What is the implication of my argument that a social life of democracy is only possible when every domain and everyday practices are democratic in nature? Are these domains obstacles to the production of this social life of democracy or do they have unique strengths to enable it?

Science, Technology and Democracy

Modern societies have been refashioned in the image of science and technology. Today, there is almost no society in the world which is not part of the global technological network. However, this does not necessarily imply that these societies are themselves scientific and modern, since their social practices may remain traditional. The use of technology today in so many practices of religion is an illustrative example of the dissonance between the values associated with science and with those of tradition and religion. Without getting into the details of this debate, I will only point out here that increasingly the theatre of conflict between science and religion is in the space of politics, particularly democratic politics. Given the focus on democracy, I will restrict my comments here to this relationship between these two domains and that of democracy, both in regards to government as well as its social life.[10]

It would not be an exaggeration to say that the notions of scientific knowledge and truth have had a great influence on public cultures of knowledge and truth. If we are to accept Ambedkar's point that democracy is about society, then a society that is deeply influenced by science and technology is also one that will influence the contemporary understanding of democracy. Moreover, science itself has to be understood as a social process. It is not only legitimized by society but also supported for the most part by governments and public money. The teaching of science has become the core of education in almost all societies today, and thus the scientific imagination wields an influence on the individual right from early childhood. Science has always been an integral part of military programmes in every country and thus has had an implicit influence on the rhetoric of nationhood. It is estimated that globally, on an average 30 to 40 per cent of government funds for science are spent on military programmes.[11] It is now an essential engine that

---

10 For a general introduction to some of the topics on the nature of science, see Sundar Sarukkai, *What Is Science?* (Delhi: National Book Trust, 2012).

11 See Congressional Research Service, 'Government Expenditures on Defense Research and Development by the United States and Other OECD Countries: Fact Sheet', 28 January 2020 (available at: https://bit.ly/3qrIHe5; last accessed on 2 September 2022); and Ministry of Science & Technology,

drives private commercial enterprise. Today, most of the money that is put into science comes from defence budgets and private entrepreneurs in the fields of pharmaceutical and chemical sciences, artificial intelligence and so on.

The nature of science has changed drastically over the last few decades, particularly after the growth of digital technologies, and this too has had a major impact on the practice of democracy around the globe. Through the spread of smartphones and data-communication technologies, the digital revolution has penetrated even those classes that had so far remained outside the purview of scientific development. In post-Independence India, politics and governance has always been influenced by big science. But now they have become more centred on science: advisors to the government, even on matters not related directly to science and technology, are drawn from the community of scientists. The increase in the amount of monetary investment from the private sector in supporting scientific research has changed the contours of the relation between the State and the scientific establishment.

Digital technology, in particular social media, has suddenly revived interest in technology's relationship with democracy. There is an inherent tension between technology and democracy because surveillance technologies and those that provide access to private information are of great help to repressive governments. However, the initial celebration of social media as an agent of democratic change has subsided and now there is a far more cautious evaluation of the impact of such technologies on the state of a country's democracy. It is indisputable that almost all these powerful technologies are produced by private companies owned

Government of India, 'Research and Development Statistics 2019–20', December 2020 (available at: https://bit.ly/3Rgr6Bh; last accessed on 2 September 2022).

by individuals or groups who possess enormous wealth and power. Thus, there is an inherent contradiction in expecting these oligarchs and their companies to be truly democratic or support democracy in their actions. Multinationals supposedly supporting democracy through their technologies are themselves not democratic in the way democracy is expected to function in societies.

At the same time, there has been a rediscovery of the connection between science and democracy. We saw this particularly during the Trump era in the United States. Almost as a reaction to his maverick pronouncements, scientists banded together to press for more science in governance. As part of this narrative, there were repeated reminders about the relationship between science and democracy. Although democracy is recognized as a political system, democratic qualities are often ascribed to the practice of science. One of those qualities—that of questioning authority—is an obvious point of commonality. It is true that the practice of science has at its core the impulse to question authoritative knowledge, but it is also clear that science as practised today is still driven by the dictates of reigning paradigms, to use Thomas Kuhn's overused term. Today, the science that is most important, as evaluated in terms of citations and impact, is being pursued and developed in private sectors—artificial intelligence, the pharmaceutical and the chemical industry, to name a few. The idea that all of science is somehow a resistance to authority is patently false.

There is, however, another aspect of scientific practice that is often connected to democracy. It has to do with the narrative of rational thought, drawing conclusions based on evidence, and being open to refutation. Although this is an ideal picture of science and remains so in its everyday practice, some elements of this description are nevertheless true. There is pressure in scientific practice to produce arguments, adduce evidence, create a space for disagreement about one's views. Many of these features have also come to stand for democratic practices, such as the importance of dissent and disagreement, formulating government policies based on evidence and properly using facts. The call to use science in the framing of public policies, such as in public health or environment sectors, has also led to a renewed engagement between science and democracy. The ideal picture of the practice of science also valorizes certain qualities such as honesty, integrity, hard work and commitment to truth. These qualities are also desirable in any government in a democratic society. Being open to criticism and using empirical knowledge in reaching decisions are aspects of scientific practice that are valuable to governance. Thus, it is not really surprising that in a world where democracy is seen to be under threat, some scientists have become more vocal in associating themselves with democratic movements. There is nevertheless an internal tension between science and democracy, a tension that has been clearly visible during the Covid-19 pandemic.

The scientific community has always been an exclusive club. The exclusionary nature need not be based on class, caste or gender—although these discriminations have always been an integral part of the scientific world, particularly in India. Exclusion here is based more on cognitive measures. There is little that is 'democratic' about scientific merit. Being good in science is a privilege afforded to the very few. The culture of competition in science means that the exclusionary practices begin very early among individuals, in many cases, right from primary school. The system of evaluation in science is biased towards certain kinds of competency, thereby keeping a majority of the population outside it.

This by itself is not a problem. What is a problem is the meaning attached to scientific knowledge, particularly in terms of its applicability in social domains. This knowledge is highly specialized and is understood by very small groups of people within each subdiscipline of science. The overspecialization of scientific disciplines has led to a proliferation of very specific domains of knowledge that are understood and interpreted by only a handful of people. Most worryingly, this knowledge is inaccessible to a large majority and, moreover, it is believed that this large majority does not have the cognitive competence to 'understand' this knowledge. So if one of the essential elements of democracy is allowing all voices to be heard, then the nature of scientific practice is, from the very start, at odds with it. However, the difference between scientific knowledge and other forms of ideological systems is that, in principle, scientific knowledge is not asserted but has to be 'proved' in some sense. Thus, the democratic impulse in science comes from the attempt to convince everybody of its knowledge claims. The success and failure of science's engagement with democracy hinge crucially on this enterprise. Popular science writing is one way to achieve this dissemination; but even though it has been greatly instrumental in promoting certain rhetoric of science, it is not capable of making scientific knowledge democratic. Forget about the general population—science education in schools has never been able to bridge this deep chasm among students between those who can 'do science' and those who are not able to. A very small section of the society produces scientific knowledge, and the access to and methods of doing so are restricted to such groups. Attempts to democratize scientific knowledge have become more of a talking-down to people. In public discussions on public health during the pandemic, it has become clear that this talking-down to the ordinary citizens is also accompanied by State and global power supported by powerful industrial interests.

The science–democracy relationship is dependent on the nature of truth itself. If truth is non-negotiable, then it becomes a mere statement of fact that has to be accepted by all. When somebody does not accept a particular scientific truth, all that a scientist can do is sit down and explain their point of view to them. While this may have still been a possibility in earlier times, it is now quite impossible. Science has changed rapidly. The production of scientific knowledge has grown exponentially. Since research publications are a measure of how much 'new' scientific knowledge is produced, it is instructive to know that the number of papers published every year runs into millions—now around eight million papers annually. If each paper is published because something 'new' is present in them, then imagine the enormous production of knowledge claims in science. What kind of knowledge is this unfathomable amount of 'new' knowledge? Almost all of it is outside the purview of ordinary citizens and in most cases outside the capacity of even scientists in other disciplines to understand and evaluate.

Private industries are also part of this production but in principle the knowledge they produce is kept secret and under intellectual property protections. Enormous amount of knowledge is produced by defence industries, chemical and pharmaceutical industries, companies that deal with information and communication technologies, most of which is not publicly accessible. And that is not only because of intellectual property restrictions but also because of the nature of that specialized knowledge. The ideal of having dialogues with citizens and attempting to convince them of the truth of science is lost under this deluge. Ironically, today science too functions as an ideology that asserts its claims and imposes them on citizens. When the public questions anything about science, including the problematic relations it has with the State or its relation to commerce and military interests, they are dubbed anti-rational and worse.

The reason that truth in science is so different from truth in politics is because of their respective natures. Scientific truths are largely about the natural world or a materially produced world. They are not about negotiations, self-abnegation or representation, all characteristics of democratic action. These are characteristics of truth in politics, a topic that I will discuss later in the book. Thus, it is not surprising that even within scientific institutions in the country, there is a dire lack of democratic norms. In India, many such institutions are top-heavy and science administration itself faces enormous challenges because it does not democratically include all the stakeholders. It is often made up of small cliques and is split across categories of region, caste and gender. There is little transparency in how major scientific projects get funded or audited. Any question on any of these practices immediately attracts the charge of being regressive, anti-rational, rightist and such. None of these exemplify any quality of democracy. There is no evaluation of science by non-scientists, even if they are professionals from other disciplines such as the social sciences. At the same time, scientists are at the forefront of decision making on many social issues just because they are scientists and not because they possess core knowledge about those situations and processes. The scientific community, in its broadest sense, has functioned through exclusion of those not in their tribe, and these practices do not encourage anyone to believe that their science has an intrinsic relationship with democracy.

Steven Shapin, in an article on science and trust, points out that historically there was an association of morality with the production of knowledge.[12] Over time and with overspecialization, a

12 Steven Shapin, 'The Way We Trust Now: The Authority of Science and the Character of the Scientists' in Pervez Hoodbhoy, Daniel Glaser and Steven

dissociation has occurred between the scientist and the moral qualities that one could expect from them.[13] Trustworthiness is one of the qualities common to both a scientist and a politician. Shapin begins by pointing out claims that there is a growing shift in the way the public responds to scientists: moving away from trusting them towards questioning what they are doing. Across all societies in the twentieth century, there has been a decline in the trust the common public puts in scientists. The impact of continuous, destructive wars driven by scientific research, as well as the public perception of the monumental changes to the environment and climate have also contributed to this shift.

Shapin argues that it is scientific expertise and technical knowledge that give scientists public authority. But the important question he poses is this: Can such expertise in itself lead to public trust? He identifies three aspects of this relationship. First, we have to trust that the person indeed has the expertise, and this we have to take on faith since knowledge now is so specialized. Second, there are many experts in every field (and this is especially true of scientific knowledge of human bodies and human societies), and there is not always a single expert voice of authority. Third, and the most important aspect, Shapin points out, knowing more is not the same as doing the right thing. Trust in expertise is not so much about how much knowledge the scientist possesses but about knowing that the expert 'means well' and will do good towards the people. This observation leads him to argue that when the public evaluates expertise, it necessarily involves a moral component.

Shapin (eds), *Trust Me: I Am a Scientist* (London: British Council, 2004), pp. 42–63.

13 For a discussion on how morality gets dissociated from modern science, see Sundar Sarukkai, 'Science and the Ethics of Curiosity', *Current Science* 97(6) (2009): 756–67.

This is a unique problem of the present times, since he notes that historically, the natural philosopher (scientist in those days) was someone who not only knew more but was also a nobler person. It is only from the late nineteenth to the early twentieth century that technical expertise slowly cut off ties to morality. The present-day social organization of science, with its dependence on the State, its ties to the military, its funding from private capitalist high-tech industries, has led to the loss of 'integrity and freedom'. After the disastrous effect of the nuclear bomb, scientists moved further away from associating themselves with a 'higher moral status', and this meant that in democratic societies at least, the authority of science and scientists had to be held accountable. But accountable to whom? This continues to be a major point of contention.

Science's romance with democracy in recent times has been catalysed more than anything else by digital technologies. The Arab Spring was a much-talked-about phenomenon and much of it had to do with an Orientalist fascination with liberating oppressed societies. But after the first honeymoon of social-media-produced visions of equal access and opportunity for all voices, the reality sank in. Digital technologies and social media have played and continue to play a major role in destabilizing democracies. The present invasion of Ukraine by Russia is driven not just by cyber war but also by conventional military technologies that are by-products of the scientific community's work. It is quite surprising that scientists do not see how the institution of science itself has been compromised by the enormous amount of money and effort put into developing war technologies. The fact that today scientific knowledge is one of the most important enablers for the invasion of a democratic country like Ukraine is yet another illustration of the troubled state of democracy in societies driven by science and technology.

And since this is the model across the world, we are going to see deeper crises of democracy unless and until the practice of science is itself made more democratic. The fundamental problem is that science, by definition, is suspicious of the intellectual capacities of the ordinary—'non-scientist'—citizen, whereas modern politics is suspicious of the citizen's moral capacities.

The counter-argument to what I have said here so far is that science is also instrumental in the progress and development of a society. Medical science has prolonged lives and material sciences have entered every household in the world in so many different ways. Even if we accept this function of technology, the question that we are concerned with is whether science can contribute to strengthening democratic qualities. Given that democracy is about human negotiations and the ethics of representation, it is less likely for science to have any direct engagement with democracy even though it may be seen to have some benefits to a larger society. If democracy is viewed as improving the lives of the poor and the marginalized, then certain technological advances can contribute to this effort. But sadly, we have seen science and technology focus very little on producing a more egalitarian society, including in India where the number of the poor and the disadvantaged continue to rise. Moreover, this does not necessarily relate to democracy, since even totalitarian governments can use these same technologies to help the poor. Thus, there is little that is intrinsic to the practice of science and democracy as such, even though scientific knowledge is necessary for proper governance as much as knowledge of the social sciences. Virtues of open-mindedness, inquisitiveness, openness to new possibilities, willingness to explore the depths of natural phenomena—these are essential qualities of a good scientist; and one can argue that these qualities are also very useful for the social life of democracy. It is thus necessary to re-energize some of these ideals of science that are rapidly losing ground in its current practices.

There is one specific consequence of technology that has a deep connection to the social life of democracy: its impact on the nature of our society and on the quality of being social. Modern-day immersion in personal gadgets such as smart-phones has made individuals far more immune to the world and to others. The image of hundreds of people in a public space such as a train or a bus or a park staring into their smartphones without even looking around them can be encountered any-where on the globe. This indifference to the other has also entered family units, and even members of a family communi-cate best through these gadgets. The pandemic of using these gadgets for everything, including fulfilling basic requirements such as getting groceries, food, and commodities of various kinds, has created a world where an individual's need to relate and engage with others has been reduced to a virtual interaction. It has also removed the sensory experience of the world and of other people. These gadgets make us live in a world we create and not in a world we inhabit. This greatly influences the idea of the social, an essential experience that makes us relate to one another as humans. Through these gadgets, we produce a society that not only just comprises individual for the most part but also one that is anonymous in character.

What happens to our ideas of democracy in this increasingly real world of the anonymous and virtual social? What really is the meaning of the public and of representative politics in this new world? What is the nature of 'We, the People' in such a society? Is this 'we' an anonymous 'we' produced through Facebook? There is no sense of the public in the individualized world in which we live inside these gadgets. We get our news and information from social media. And thanks to the pandemic, we do not even see the people who bring to our doorsteps what we order online. We meet invisible friends and make passionate enemies of people we do not know or will ever meet. All this is dumped on us at such a rapid pace that there is no moment to pause, no collective ways to think about the impact of all these technologies. A sense of the public comes through our experience of the social, through social relations and socially meaningful action. These are catalysed only through our engagement and negotiation with others. In this sense, given the importance of negotiations, the social is already political. One might argue that we do engage with others even in the virtual medium when we read and respond to news and comments on social media. But this is not an engagement with others. As Guru and I argued in our book *Experience, Caste and the Everyday Social*, the social is grounded in sensory experiences of sound, smell, touch, taste and sight. The social is produced from these experiences. When we interact with others, we operate sensorially. In the virtual world, the sensory domain is lost and we access only a deformed visual spectacle. Thus, the creation of the anonymous social through these technologies has led to a society without a sense of the public and hence without a sense of democracy. All that is left of democracy is some naive idea of individual choice and individual freedom.

These technologies actually go far beyond just seducing the individual into an anonymous social. They also intervene in very dangerous ways in democratic principles. The countless examples of anti-democratic and authoritarian use of digital media must concern us deeply. Today, this has expanded to new levels through unregulated practices involving cryptocurrencies, Web 3.0 and such. Enormous power rests in the hands of a few techno-entrepreneurs with very little accountability. We are self-delusional if we think that these developments actually promote democracies across the globe. One can respond by arguing that rather than seeing the demise of democracy in this new tech age, we can instead consider it as a reconfiguration of democracy in an anonymous, digital social world. However, given the oligarchic and inherently capitalist nature of production of these technologies, along with the lack of democratic practices in the everyday life in these domains, it is not clear how new forms of democracy could emerge from them.

Religion and Democracy

Modern societies are deeply impacted by science and technology but they are also increasingly coming under the explicit influence of religion as a social institution. This has always been true of India, and the emphasis on scientific temper and industrial culture after Independence was a visible attempt to reduce the impact of religion on our society. What do these changing relations bode for democracy? As in the case of science, the literature on religion and society is vast and what I want to do here is to focus on a specific relation between religion and the notion of democracy. In this brief discussion, what I want to do is to argue that just as the ideal qualities of scientific practice are important for the cultivation of a democratic self so too are some ideal qualities of religion. These ideal qualities in the context of science are necessary to the practice of knowledge production (how to know?) whereas the ideal qualities of religion play an important role in social life and for human action (how to live?).

Why should religion matter to a discussion on democracy? Like most other concepts that have been discussed here, there are many meanings that can be ascribed to religion. The word 'religion' might mean ideas of faith, belief in god, norms of morality, rituals of culture and so on. There are many different religions, and concepts such as faith and god have different implications in each of them. My analysis is going to be restricted to one specific point—Ambedkar's intriguing comment about the relation between religion and democracy. I focus on this because the larger project of this book is to exhibit the contours of the social life of democracy, in consonance with an Ambedkarite vision of democracy.

Ambedkar's view on Hinduism is well known and is most poignantly captured by his powerful statement that even though he was born a Hindu, he would not die one. His trenchant criticism of Hinduism was based on the argument that the caste system is intrinsic to Hinduism and his project of annihilation of caste quite obviously meant the full-scale rejection of Hinduism. However, he was also aware of the importance of religion in social life—for, after all, towards the end of his life he and his followers converted to another 'religion', Buddhism. Even though these facts are well known, what is perhaps not as well understood is his argument linking democracy to religion. We have seen already that for Ambedkar there is no possibility of democracy without fraternity. But where does fraternity come from? How does one inculcate feelings of fraternity in human beings?[14] In Riddle 22 of his 'Riddles in Hinduism', Ambedkar asks: 'Wherein lie the roots of fraternity without which Democracy is not possible?' He answers thus: 'Beyond dispute, it has its origin in Religion.'[15]

---

14 It is instructive to see how Charles Taylor tries to understand 'fraternity' in contrast to Ambedkar's interpretation. This difference captures an important distinction in the way Western societies have, in general, tried to understand democracy in terms of institutions. See Charles Taylor, 'The Meaning of Secularism', *The Hedgehog Review* 12(3) (Fall 2010): 23–34. I thank Srinivasan Ramanujam for discussions related to this point.

15 Ambedkar, 'Riddles in Hinduism', p. 284. Quotes in the following paragraph are from the same source, pp. 284–6.

The context of this utterance is also important. Ambedkar wants to know why democracy did 'not grow in India'. He says it is because 'Hindu Religion does not teach fraternity. Instead it teaches division of society into classes or varnas and the maintenance of separate class consciousness. In such a system where is the room for Democracy?' But it would not be true to say, he continues, that there is no space for democracy within Hindu thought: 'The Hindu Religious and Philosophic thought gave rise to an idea which had greater potentialities for producing social democracy than the idea of fraternity. It is the doctrine of Brahmaism.' Brahmaism is a term which, he mentions in a footnote, he takes from Edward Washburn Hopkins. Ambedkar's argument about Brahmaism is persuasive. The foundational pillar of Vedantic thought are the three mahavakyas: All is Brahma, I am Brahma, Thou art Brahma. Ambedkar refers to these three expressions as Brahmaism that is distinct from Vedanta as well as Brahmanism. He locates the difference as follows: 'Brahmaism and Vedanta agree that Atman is the same as Brahma. But the two differ in that Brahmaism does not treat the world as unreal, Vedanta does.' He then uses this formulation to argue that Brahmaism, which he refers to as 'the most democratic principle', has the potential to ground democracy in Hindu thought. He argues that not only can it provide a foundation but also make democracy obligatory for all because it leads to the realization that 'you and I are parts of the same cosmic principle' which 'leaves room for no other theory of associated life except democracy'. He extends this argument to add that India too produced a 'theoretical foundation of democracy' through this doctrine. The riddle for him is that even though Hinduism seemed to have had the philosophical foundation for democracy and equality so forcefully expressed in the mahavakyas, these principles did not become the 'basis for dharma' nor did they destroy the inequalities between various groups in Hindu society. We can see a similar invocation of the principles of non-duality in another important social reformer of caste, Narayana Guru.[16]

Keeping these thoughts as a guiding principle, I will discuss one aspect of the relationship between religion and democracy. On the surface, there are important similarities between the two. Both are forms of social life, have an inbuilt theory of equality in them, are associated with particular forms of labour, and have similar problems in the way the ideal gets translated into institutions. Furthermore, both expect a transformation of the individual self, have principles of self-abnegation at work, and have an essential relation to trust and faith. I will very briefly discuss each of these points and end with a discussion on the question of faith and autonomy. Given that religion as a term has many different meanings, I want to be careful to dissociate the social practice and institutionalization of religion from the aspect I will focus on: its foundational impulses.

Religion is an essential component of social life, especially in Asia and Africa. The engagement with religion occurs at multiple levels and with different faiths, and is not reducible to daily rituals or visits to holy places. Religions also provide their followers with codes of conduct in social settings, including moral codes. The riddle, as enunciated by Ambedkar in the context of Hinduism, can be broadened to ask: Why then do religious communities allow for unequal and undemocratic practices in society?

Religions contain foundational themes that are related to democracy. One such is the presence of a transcendent being.

---

16 For more on this, see Guru and Sarukkai, *Experience, Caste and the Everyday Social.*

One might argue that belief in such a superior being in whose eyes all human beings are equal immediately creates the possibility of democracy. There are three problems with this argument: one, disagreements on the existence of such a being; and two, the being might actually legitimize inequality among humans as in the case of caste system; and three, equality in the eyes of this being is not enough to ensure equality of humans in the world that humans inhabit. Perhaps it is this kind of reasoning that makes Ambedkar assert that saying we are all 'children of god' is a 'weak foundation' for democracy. A democracy based on such an idea will be shaky in nature. Nevertheless, an extra-human entity provides a possible philosophical ground for negating hierarchies between humans. But the question is how that might be translated into social practice. Ambedkar accepts such a transcendent term when he notes that the realization that all human beings are part of the same cosmic principle 'does not merely preach Democracy. It makes democracy an obligation of one and all.'[17] Of course, this opens up the space for exploring what this 'cosmic principle' could be and how it is related to religion as such, since Ambedkar is making this point in the context of Brahmaism.

In the context of democracy, I argued earlier that the notion of labour is absolutely essential. This notion becomes important in the context of religion too. There are two major forms of labour that arise in the practice and discourse of religion. An important functional principle of religion is that god has the capability to 'do' work on 'one's behalf'. How we interpret this depends on various religious doctrines. But whether it be the labour of comfort and protection or the greater labour of 'liberation' and 'saving', god has the capacity to labour on our

---

17 Ambedkar, 'Riddles in Hinduism', p. 286.

behalf. At the same time, there is also the labour of the believer and the kinds of work that she needs to do to keep her faith. In a sense, the worlds of gods and humans are arranged according to these forms of labour, just like human society is. And there is a clearly built hierarchy in these forms of labour.

Both religion and democracy additionally have the specific task of transforming the individual self. We saw earlier that producing the social life of democracy is to produce a democratic self. Religious beliefs and practices operate on the self in various ways. It produces qualities of humility as well as arrogance, equality of being but hierarchy of existence (a classic instance being the view that the soul and the self do not have caste and gender associations but the human being in which these are located do), and inspires transformations in individuals in regard to how they understand themselves in relation to god and to others. But is religion able to transform selves so as to produce democratic selves? And if it does have the capacity to do so, would religion be acceptable as a functioning agent of democracy? All that we can say now is that conceptually religion might have the power to produce democratic selves but institutionally they have not been able to do so.

Religion and democracy are also deeply related to the notions of truth and faith. If a voter trusts that a politician will do the job expected of her, so too does a believer trust that she will be 'protected' by god. Is the notion of trust in both these domains similar or different? What kinds of trust drive democracy, which involves trusting the actions of others? And what kinds drive religion, which has to do with trusting the divine? These questions have been integral to various philosophical traditions and here I merely state them out to show that the social life of democracy is a life that has to engage with questions of religion as a form of social life and how it deals with religion will itself define the nature of that democracy.

There is another theme that lies at the core of democratic politics and religion. This is the theme of self-abnegation, of voluntarily giving up something of one's own. In the practices of both democracy and religion, one gives up one's individual autonomy to another out of volition. As I will argue in the latter part of the book, voting is a way of giving away our right to rule to another. In religion, there is an inherent tension between totally giving in to faith and asserting one's autonomy to follow that faith. When representatives of religion begin to protect their gods, then they are fundamentally asserting their autonomy over that of their gods. Even religious mystics have always had moments of deep doubt about their faith, and in these states they struggle with their autonomy to decide against following that faith. In general, it is reasonable to argue that faith is related to trust and to surrendering oneself to another. The notion of surrendering oneself to god exists in all religions. But there arises this quandry: Is it the individual who makes the decision to surrender, in which case the agency to surrender is still with the individual and not with god? Or is it that the labour of god (god's work) is to lead the followers to surrender? These questions have been widely discussed in all religions, and extending these to truth and faith in democracy is not too far-fetched. Because in both these cases, what is at stake is the autonomous giving-up of our autonomy. We decide to act in a manner that removes ourselves as agents of that action. In democracy, when we voluntarily give up our claims to public wealth in which we have a share so that somebody else can manage it, we are, of our own volition, choosing somebody to rule over us. More than anything else, this complex engagement with our own autonomy and what we decide to autonomously do with it actually brings democracy closer to religion than to other domains. One concept in which both have invested very heavily is freedom. For all religions, the promise of ultimate freedom—liberation, moksha—is one of the most important elements of their doctrines. And in an odd way, freedom has come to stand as a most important value in modern societies. Although the concept of freedom has the potential to introduce an important ethical element into democracy, it has been diluted and has become more a term of entitlement. The role of religion in democracy also signals the difficulty in formulating ethical principles that underlie democratic action. In the next chapter, I discuss some of these underlying principles.

4.

THE ETHICAL PROCESSES OF DEMOCRACY

Ambedkar's notion of democracy based on equality, liberty and fraternity explicitly brings in certain ethical elements into the notion of democracy. Too much has been invested in the end product of democracy. Elections and institutions like the parliament, the bureaucracy and so on have been the focus of democracy. But these are the end products of democracy, and by focusing on these end products, undemocratic processes within them often remain hidden. Such an approach towards democracy tends to lead to the view that if the end product of a system is good for the people and works towards the welfare of the people, then the system can be called democratic. This is the strategy in the use of the word democratic to describe governments which would otherwise be called authoritarian or dictatorship. Focusing on the end product would be a restricted view of democracy since the essence of democracy lies in the processes that lead to the end product. There is a strong correlation with the ethics of means and ends in this process. It is not possible to value an end if the means towards that end are unethical. Processes of democracy must capture the life of democracy. I will illustrate this point by discussing the nature of voting, since so much of the performance of democracy has been reduced to voting. Although one might think of voting as a particular process of politics, there are intrinsic democratic qualities of the individual that the act demands. Being more aware of these qualities is important for the production of our democratic selves as well as for articulating the ethical dimensions of democracy.

Voting in itself is not a complete representation of democracy. As discussed in the last chapter, the question that we need to ask is about the nature of the labour of voting and the labour of participating in political democracy. The processes of elections and voting need other elements to make them democratic processes. As mentioned earlier, it is well known that political parties often pay money to voters or give 'freebies' before an election. This practice has become so common that it is no longer done in secret. Politicians visit houses in public view and distribute money and material goods like clothes, electrical appliances and so on. The public as well as political commentators often point to these aspects as the limitations of Indian democracy. However, we need to understand the implications of this process and in what sense the act of voting is 'democratic'.

It is possible to identify certain processes of public and social action that have the qualities of being democratic. The first point to note is that voting is primarily a transaction. It is a unique type of transaction. Although it seems restricted to the domain of politics, this type of transaction occurs often in everyday life. But then, what is special to the transaction inherent in voting? The transaction in political democracy is the willing transfer of what we jointly 'own' to somebody else to manage and govern. The will of the people that is often emphasized in democracy is actually little more than an action of individuals to willingly give what is theirs—namely, the public wealth in which all the people have a share—to somebody else to govern. This is the broadest understanding of democracy as a political process. Politicians primarily get elected to manage public wealth and the larger society on behalf of others. This is primarily a transaction because the 'public' is a domain common to all, commonly owned by all, but which can only be governed by a few. So all democratic governance is a governance 'on behalf of', 'in lieu of', 'in place of'. Governance-on-behalf-of in order to increase the comfort and well-being of the citizens. Therefore, we come back to the question we discussed earlier: whether a government that does 'well' by its people is more democratic than one that has the qualities of a 'free' democracy but does less for its people? The fundamental problem in viewing democracy as governance-on-behalf-of is that it allows for benign authoritarianism, where the 'ruler' can claim that the authoritarian system is democratic because it is a benign authority which functions for the good of the people. Dictatorships and politically repressive governments have often taken recourse to this argument. Even the Chinese claim to democracy discussed earlier stresses this aspect.

This is a genuine problem: If a government is more sensitive to the plight of the poor and the marginalized, and improves the quality of life for these segments, should it matter that they be elected as defined in particular models of democracy? If democratic governance does not lead to social justice, for example, is it a better system than that which works towards social justice and social emancipation? Communist regimes have often called themselves democratic in this spirit of democracy, namely, a system that works towards the betterment of all in a society, particularly the poor and the working class. Such models of democracy are not too different from the model of a benign father of the family, which gets extended to the benign patriarch of institutions and governments.

So what are the essential qualities of democracy that are important? If democratic qualities are not evaluated only in terms of their final effect on people, then benign dictatorships cannot be called a democracy. Even the phrase 'good for the people' is fraught with problems. What is 'good for the people'? Who decides this? The people themselves? Individually? Collectively? As a majority? Through voting? Does 'good for the people' entail good for *all* the members in this group? Since this is quite impossible, it would be easier to define 'good for the people' not as a general abstract idea or one that is reducible to every individual, but as larger goods—such as public goods and economic goods. For example, one could say that allowing access to health and education for all is definitely good for the people. Having a free-market choice of consumer goods is often presented as something that is good for the people, but the poor may prefer basic access to health and education to consumer choice of material goods. Therefore, 'good for the people' does not guarantee democracy unless the nature of this 'good' is more clearly defined. In public discourse on this subject, we often come across terms like 'freedom' as a measure of the 'good for the people'. Independent of access to health and education, or even consumer goods, the idea of freedom has become central to public articulations of democracy.

One of the core ethical rules that legitimizes democracy is the argument of the greatest good. It is impossible to satisfy the needs of *all* the people. So whom does democracy really try to satisfy? Any evaluation of democracy has to be based on the answer to this question. Today, democracy seems to have worked well for the growing middle class in India as far as consumer choice is concerned. But at the same time, there has also been a downward trend in the political consciousness among this group. What distinguishes democracy from other forms of benign governance are not just the notions of freedom and liberty but a far more important ethical principle. The idea of 'the People' has never been entirely inclusive as many have been kept out of this category for various reasons. If the term 'the People' has to have any ethical meaning (and not just be a quantitative measure), it can only be one that is defined from the perspective of the worst-off in society rather than from the standpoint of the elite or even the majority. *Thus, the only meaningful evaluation of democracy has to primarily be with respect to governance for the well-being of the worst-off in society.* This is an ethical stance special to democracy and it does not depend on the greatest good argument unless the worst-off is in the majority in a society, in which case it is indeed a sad society. A democracy has rarely been 'by the People'. It has benefited sections within a society, and in general the rich in democratic countries have become richer. And sometimes, the poor too have been pulled out of their conditions. But there has always been a surplus of the poor who are left behind in every democracy as well as growing inequality between the poor and the rich. In fact, we have to confront the uncomfortable fact that the percentage of the poor in a democracy has not drastically decreased over time even as its overall wealth and the wealth of a certain percentage of its population has increased. So, definitely, democracy as we see in practice today has not been for 'the People'. It has only been a successful model for a segment of the people and has escaped accountability by creating a myth of 'the People' as if that includes all the people in a society.

While the greatest-good argument is very popular and seems reasonable when dealing with the conflicting aims and interests of a huge population, it can be critiqued on many grounds. The foremost is the question of whether it indeed is the 'greatest good'. To define it in this manner, we have to show that particular acts are indeed for the greatest good but in most cases this never happens. Moreover, such a claim might be relevant to all political systems and is not restricted to democracy alone. The ethical core of democracy cannot lie in the greatest-good argument. Rather, it lies in always acting autonomously on behalf of the worst-off, the marginalized, the voiceless and the powerless in society. It is only through this definition that democracy becomes part of daily life and becomes a form of social order rather than just a political one. It is through these qualities of the social life of democracy that one can truly build a democratic society. Democratic governance is a constant evaluation of priorities in order to keep this principle as the defining principle. Given that this should be the ideal of democracy, what kind of ethical issues are conceptually relevant for understanding democracy in many of the Asian and African societies?

I will consider ethical actions corresponding to democratic processes by analysing processes such as voting, policies such as reservation, and creating an experience of the public instead of just starting with an assumption of the public. I isolate these themes because much of the public discourse on democracy often exhibits confusion about the function and the meaning of these processes, particularly that of voting.

The Ethical Act of Voting[1]

There are some standard public narratives about voting in India. The better-off groups do not participate in elections as actively as those worse off than them. The upper classes claim that the

---

1 This section is a modified and edited version of my op-ed pieces in the newspaper *The Hindu*, titled 'Ethical Act of Voting' (18 April 2019) and 'What's in an Election?' (22 May 2018).

poor vote only in order to get various benefits such as money, consumer goods, clothes and so on. The majority claims that the minorities vote as a bloc with the added suggestion that this voting is primarily influenced by considerations of religious identity. These acts are seen to represent the weaknesses in Indian democracy. Not so surprisingly, these have also led to various recipes for improving democracy, such as potential restrictions on who can vote and sometimes even suggesting that the British should be brought back to rule India! These electoral practices, combined with money and muscle power, which are needed to survive elections and party politics, show Indian democracy in a poor light. They also seem to suggest that it is impossible for voters to function as responsible individuals for they are not doing their duty of voting for the best person, namely, the best political representative who will govern well. Much of this is based on the belief that there is a particular purpose to voting which many do not adhere to in their act of voting. Whether it is voting for money or voting based on caste or religious considerations, these voters are seen to go against the purpose of voting in a democracy. Of course, one can extend this argument to everybody who votes: some may vote for a party based on certain ideological principles, others based on expectations of some economic policies that they support and so on. Every act of voting is based on some expectation and so is always a transaction, a social transaction. On the other hand, while these problems about elections are generally true in national and more centralized political processes, democracy when decentralized has not only had a significant impact but has also been more socially sensitive.

It is often said that voting is a duty, but what kind of duty is it? Is it to make a choice on a sheet or is it actually a particular process of thinking and deciding? Moreover, if it is a duty, then duty to whom? To whom is the voter accountable? Although democracy seems to highlight the role of a voter as an autonomous agent, every voter recognizes that their vote is only a negligible fraction of the thousands of other votes that are cast. So when they vote they are playing a guessing game, since there is no direct correlation between one individual's vote and the potential outcome of the election. It is the pragmatics of this game of making the best possible guess that drives voters to indulge in transactions with politicians. Consider the act of voting by those who get paid before they vote. In taking money or goods, voters see elections as a transaction. What they are basically asking is this: What am I getting in return for voting for you? This transactional mode is a natural consequence as long as the voters see the elected representative using their election to increase their power and individual wealth. Voters ask this question because they have seen for decades after independence that becoming an elected politician has led to a massive increase in the wealth of that politician and their family. So if voting has to be disinterested—in the sense of not expecting benefit for oneself by voting—then it should also be the case that those who are governing should also be disinterested in personal benefit. But when governance has become a business for the politicians, why should the voter not demand their price? In fact, the transactional mode of voting shows clearly the wisdom of the voters who have recognized the empty claims that democracy is for 'the People'. Thus, the voter thinks that she is doing a job for a politician whom she votes for and expects to get paid for that act. So also, the politician understands the business aspect of voting very well and is willing to spend money as an investment for future profit. This is the dilemma in electing somebody, a dilemma that is so well understood by the public. They argue that as voters they are supposed to vote for free, whereas the result of their action ends up creating power and wealth for another person. So why is voting not seen as a business transaction when the winner of the election profits from the action of the voter? Why can't the voter who is enabling opportunity for another person's wealth ask for a share in that wealth? In fact, this argument is a perfectly rational one from the voter's side. On the other side, there is a similar rationale for the politician: they pay the voters since giving money to voters is like an investment. The amount voters are paid is a measure of how much elected representatives hope to make during their tenure!

But there is also an underlying belief that such actions do not constitute democracy. In the case of an ideal democracy, what would be the nature and function of voting? The fundamental difference between the social model of democracy that I discussed above and voting today is that in the former, voting is not an act that will yield personal benefit but one that will improve the well-being of others who are worse off. For those who are better off in a society, their vote is not a vote for their self-interest but a vote for the interests of those worse off than them. For those in the lowest stratum, if they do get to vote, then their vote is to improve their basic well-being. If we agree that democracy should always be defined relationally with respect to the worst-off, we cannot define the voting by that group as voting for self-interest.

The dynamics of voting is thus a complex problem of rationality, similar to problems in rational choice theory. First, how do politicians know that the people will vote for them after taking their money or listening to their promises, especially if more than one politician pays the same group of people or makes similar promises? Moreover, how do they know that enough people will vote for them to make them win? For the voter, it is a much simpler calculation. They get paid for a service they perform by voting and they can maximize the benefit they get from different parties. Interestingly, many of them apparently do vote for the person they take money from, because they feel they are *morally* bound to do so. But once money is transferred, there are other factors that influence voting, including fear. There is a problem when voting is reduced to this monetary transaction, because then democracy gets reduced to principles of business. In such a case, the government will literally be in the 'business of running the country'. But for real democracy to be possible, voting has to be seen as something more than a transaction and more as an ethical duty. It might be useful to remember that benefit for the larger society will include others benefiting as much as each one of us through our votes. That is, when I vote, I vote on behalf of others who are worse off than me and not on behalf of myself. This duty is the ethical rationality of democratic voting.

Trusteeship

Another essential ethical concept related to democracy is trusteeship. Trusteeship is an important idea that has a direct relation to governance and democracy but often escapes the scrutiny of theories of democracy. Trusteeship is also a concept that extends democratic principles into various other social domains, including that of business. Philanthropy is built on the principles of trusteeship. Elections too have a direct relationship to the ideal of trusteeship, and this gives another ethical foundation to elections.

In the above section, I argued that voting in a democracy implies a duty to vote for the betterment of others. This claim is also supported by the way we understand the primary purpose of a democratic election. Elections are fundamentally a way to make the elected accountable to the people, to those who do not wield that power. They are a means towards the goal of controlling those who wield power. All other features that are commonly associated with democracy, such as freedom of speech and freedom of the media, are primarily methods to attain this goal. But today, elections have become an end in themselves.

There is a fundamental paradox present in voting somebody to political power. First of all, what is the intention behind voting for somebody? Voting is important as a democratic process because of an underlying assumption about public wealth. The original idea of 'We, the People' comes not from legal belongingness to a State or of being part of a group or community. Rather, it comes from a recognition that the people own something together. They are shareholders of the public space. Like shareholders of a company, they do not need to have socially associated relationships between them. 'We, the People' is produced through a sense of ownership more than a sense of belonging. From this sense of ownership, other possible social relationships can develop. So what is it that the people own? In modern nations, which develop a sense of public property in contrast to private property, 'the People' are equal owners of the public wealth. Every public space is legitimately owned equally by the people. A modern democratic society is one that is not owned by one monarch or by one dictator. Although there is private wealth, including private ownership of land, there is a large amount of public space that in principle belongs to the public. It belongs in equal measure to all the people who have a claim to that public domain. All people have an equal claim to the public goods in the society they belong to. A public park is public only because the park is 'owned' by all the people in equal measure. This means that, in principle, the poorest person in a society has an equal share in the public wealth as the richest person.

Voting and in general democratic processes have to be understood through this prism of shared ownership. Land is a particularly important and valuable commodity, and many who enter politics have profited from usurping public land as their own. A politician is voted to administer the land and, as extension, all the wealth that belongs to the public but he does so only *on behalf of* the other owners, namely, the people. Thus, we vote because we have a say in the public wealth and we choose somebody to administer that wealth on our behalf. When we vote somebody to power, we are not giving that person 'power' to do what they want but we are merely choosing a person to take care of the public wealth that belongs equally to all of us. Electing someone is merely choosing a representative to take care of our share of the public domain, and nothing more than that. The true act of democracy lies not just in how this job is done by the elected representatives but in making them accountable for this job. This is the ideal, even though we are far removed from ideal mechanisms that can enforce this accountability. In India, elections once in five years are the most obvious manifestation of this accountability but even this has been compromised because of a misrepresentation of what elections really stand for.

This ideal is nothing but the principle of trusteeship that was so forcefully articulated by Gandhi and which even influenced businessmen like J. R. D. Tata.[2] Gandhi's idea of trusteeship was that we don't own our wealth but only have control of it in so far as we operate it as a trust for the betterment of others. This is a radical idea propounded by Gandhi, and

2 For more on this, see Sundar Sarukkai, *JRD Tata and the Ethics of Philanthropy* (London and New York: Routledge, 2020).

although J. R. D. Tata, one of India's pioneering and successful businessmen, disagreed with some of the principles of trusteeship enunciated by Gandhi, he nevertheless followed the idea of trusteeship in his own business practice. The Tatas continue to remain one of the most trusted brands in India in large part due to these ethical foundations of their business practices.

In the domain of democratic politics, trusteeship is a most important principle. What this means is that the elected representatives function merely trustees on behalf of the people and it is the primary duty of the trustee to make sure that they do not destroy what they are trustees of. This is a meaningful and powerful implication of democracy, and it is precisely this character of democracy that has been destroyed in viewing elections purely as an instrumental end of democracy. The rules of trusteeship that Gandhi lists may seem to be impractical but there have been attempts by many individuals and groups to live by at least some of these principles. In politics, trusteeship can be understood as the demand that a government should function like a Trust. There are two important principles intrinsic to the idea of a Trust. One, a person can put all their money into a Trust but in principle she does not have complete authority over what is done with it. Two, there are external systems that the Trust will be answerable to so as to make sure that the money is not misused. This idea of a Trust challenges well-entrenched ideas about a person's relationship to her wealth. In a consumerist society, the entrenched view is that an individual can do what she wants with 'her' money. Trusteeship challenges this problematic claim about ownership of one's wealth. One way to understand this challenge is to recognize that both money and the idea of an individual are socially produced and sanctioned terms. Therefore, in any invocation of the phrase 'my money', the social is already present.

Democracy has at its foundations a deep relationship with the ethical notion of trust. When we vote, we vote based on the trust that the person who is going to represent us will indeed represent us fairly and govern justly. The quality of trust is an important glue of human relations. Whatever the disagreements a child may have with their parents, her existence is based on a fundamental and unquestionable trust in the adults around her. Betrayal of trust is a betrayal that is among the most heinous. Trust is not just an ideal value but also of great pragmatic use. We can continue with our everyday lives without worrying at each point because we trust that others will do what they are expected to do. There are different types of trust; a child's trust in her parents is not the trust that is integral to democracy or politics. Nevertheless, they share some basic qualities that make the larger idea of trust an important governing principle of democracy itself. It is trust that is also necessary for producing 'fellow-feeling', the requirement that Ambedkar forces on democracy.

If democracy is dependent on an expression of trust, then good governance is possible primarily as a form of trusteeship. What the elected representatives are supposed to do is to 'govern' only in so far as they are true to their task of governing on behalf of the public. To so govern is to take decisions and implement them so as to protect the common public goods in which all have an equal share. But most often, instead of being trustees, elected representatives take a share of the public wealth for their personal gain, thereby leading to a violation of this trust. What is needed in such a case is to inculcate democratic practices into all domains of society (as discussed in an earlier chapter) and to consciously produce discourses explaining the ideas of trustee-ship in the context of governance. In the previous section when I argued that voting should be on behalf of others worse off, it was an expression of trusteeship that is forced upon us as democratic citizens. Being in a democracy, the question of trusteeship is applicable not only to the elected. It is also applicable to each one of us who vote. When we vote to improve the well-being of the worse-off, each one of us is acting as a trustee of our society. In such a case, to vote democratically would mean that one would vote for policies that benefit the poor and the excluded independent of the impact of these policies on the individual who votes. This is what democracy means and this is how a meaningful idea of 'the People' can be produced.

Unless democracy becomes part of everyday social life, governance will be an exotic Other for the people. This is another way of stating that political democracy is not possible if the constituents of that political structure are undemocratic. It is also the case that the absence of a true sense of democracy in politics influences every other aspect of society. Few of our institutions imbibe a sense of democratic functioning in this true sense. Private institutions anyway make little pretence of democracy since the private, by definition, has little sense of the shared trusteeship of the public. But we can demand some ethical conduct from the private because even the private needs a stable public space to enable its existence. But whether in politics or in institutions which claim to be democratic, the demand is for much more than mere rituals of choice present in voting. That can only happen when it is power that is democratized, and not choice alone. While all of us recognize that sharing power democratically is difficult even in small organizations, let alone the government, we should also be aware that as long as the intentions of the person wielding power is that of a trustee, there is at least the potential to be democratic.

Moreover, when the act of being democratic is reduced to only that of voting, then it follows that the people who vote belong to the political process only at the moment they vote.

Once they finish voting, they no longer have any place in the democratic process. Any process that does this has no hope of truly being democratic. This is what has led to the deep sense of political alienation among the people. It is this political alienation which often leads to cultural alienation, which in turn leads to polarizing movements based on hate and hierarchy. So the challenge is to imagine a democratic process that will make voting a true representative of the ideals of trusteeship and to have a process that will demand democratic actions not just of the elected but also of those who cast the vote. And that is possible only when we view democracy as a form of social life.

Creating an Experience of the 'Public'

In the previous section, I argued that modern ideas of democracy are closely tied in with notions of sharing and administering public wealth. Thus, the concept of the public itself plays an important part in a discourse of democracy. But what is this public? Is it a given? Is it another synonym for 'the People'? Earlier, I discussed the rhetorical function of 'the People' and the myth that it has become. In this chapter, I suggested that one way to understand the formation of the public was through the common wealth that is shared by all. But it would be a mistake to assume that there is always a given public. Rather, I would argue that the creation of a public is one of the most important tasks for democracy. There is no given public as such and anti-democratic governments do their best to stop the production of the public. The creation of a public is an extremely important product of democracy and this process is an ethical imperative for democracy. In the context of Western modernity, Habermas' formulation of the public sphere has had a wide currency. The public sphere has been most dominantly associated with communicative practices of people expressing free opinion and discussing solutions. It largely emphasises communication in the society. My arguments for the production of the public is slightly different and is a response to the question of what the notion of the public could be now given the politics of the times. Such a public arises from ethical imperatives rather than as an off-shoot of particular social processes.

Societies are not naturally associated with the sense of a public. Societies can be formed on the basis of caste, religion, language and so on, but in none of them is a sense of the public necessary. Thus, a sense of the public and of 'the People' have to be first created through democratic action. Therefore, democracy in societies that do not have a well-formed idea of the public has to be understood as social actions that will lead to an articulation of the public and produce experiences of being part of a public. That should be the foremost work of democracy in such societies. This problem of producing new publics is not just a problem in Asian and African societies; increasingly, it has become one in Western societies too. New mechanisms for producing the sense of 'we' are needed to accommodate the changing demographics in these societies and such experiences of the public can no longer be supported only by institutional and legal means. Communicative praxis alone is not enough.

Today, one often understands the idea of public as a term that is in opposition to the notion of private. And this opposition has come to be largely understood in terms of economic ownership. The public has come to be associated almost completely with the government and the private with corporate and business enterprises. But it is important to recover the larger and essential meaning of public which is related to an important facet of a democratic society. In brief, the first and true function of democracy is to produce a public, a sense of the public and an experience of the public. What could this actually mean?

What really is the public? Is it just another collection of 'all people'? This is not a useful definition of the public. I begin with the point that a public is not a mere collection of many people and many strangers. One of the most powerful ideas of the public is present in the commonly used term 'public space'. But this space has to be understood not merely as one which has no restrictions and which is open to all who want to enter it. These qualities of access are important but they are more a consequence of a deeper foundational principle. There are two possible meanings to the idea of public: one is based on the idea of *inclusion*, which is the space which anybody can access; the other is based on the notion of *not-exclusion*, that is a space that does not exclude anybody. In simple binary logic, we would see these two terms as being the same but it is not so when they are viewed as social processes. So we can consider a deeper meaning of the public as follows: the public is the production of conditions which will accommodate not merely those who can be part of that space but also those who are not welcome in that space. This is a negative definition of the public and is different from merely saying that a public space accommodates all. Accommodating all is not the goal that relates the idea of the public to democracy. *A democratic public only arises when conditions are created to share spaces with those we are different from, those we do not necessarily like and those we disagree with.*

Cultures are often spaces of exclusion and a society as such cannot legislate these exclusions. People of similar class, caste and religion may prefer to stay together. So a social space is marked by these differences and, in a sense, is only an extension of private space, which, by definition, allows access only to those whom the owners of that space want. A private space allows the luxury of deciding who will be allowed entry. A public space is exactly the opposite but it is also not enough to say that it can allow all. If there is a space that allows strangers, but strangers who are 'like us', then it is not really a public space. This phenomenon is now extremely common; public spaces including parks are more and more occupied by people who are 'comfortable' with the presence of others. When they encounter people who dress differently or talk in different languages, there is an immediate reaction. The democratic sense of the public arises in conditions that are uncomfortable and that force individuals to be in uncomfortable group settings. Thus, the public has to be defined negatively—not as a set of conditions allowing access but as conditions that will allow access to those who are not seen to be welcome in that space. Extending this definition, I pointed out in an essay on protest that

> Public space is commonly understood as a place that is 'open' to all, but this view does not capture the most important function of this space. All these spaces are only 'potentially open' to all; in reality there are various types of restrictions and obstacles. I would define a public space as one in which we have necessarily to share space with people we don't like and with those who would not be welcomed into private spaces such as homes. It is this spirit of being forced to share, to be 'decent' to others independent of one's 'right' to dislike others, that is the mark of a public space. Such a space is a necessary condition for protest. A public space (such as a park) seen only as a place for leisure, exercise, entertainment or other social gatherings is not a true public space if it is not a space conducive to protest.[3]

---

3 Sundar Sarukkai, 'Voice and the Metaphysics of Protest', *Postcolonial Studies* 24(1) (2021): 4–10.

Democracy is much more than a matter of governance. Its very engagement with the idea of the 'the People' is not guaranteed by a Constitution or by having elections. The notion of 'the People' arises first through the notion of the public. And democracy's fundamental role is to produce experiences of the public. The public that is produced by democracy is firstly an experience. Democracy produces an experience of the notion of the public which is very different from other experiences that also involve a collective, such as a group experience of a religious ritual or the experience of following similar social norms as in a particular caste group. In other words, it is not enough to say that one is part of the public. It is more important to produce experiences that create a feeling of being part of a public. It is this feeling that is the first step in producing the feeling of fraternity that Ambedkar talks about.

The experience of the public is essential because it is this experience that functions as a ground for our notions of the public, of collective belonging. A public space that is produced democratically allows entry to all and, in particular, guarantees entry to those who may not be otherwise welcome in such a space. We learn about the nature of the public from our experiences that characterize the public. This experience is important because it is also integral to our recognition of becoming 'We, the People'. And the ideals of democracy are closely linked to this recognition since the governance of the people needs a prior understanding of how we are part of one entity called 'the People'.

So what would constitute the experience of the public which is a necessary condition to understand and experience what it means to be democratic, for what it means to understand democracy as a way of life? Group experience is not the experience of the public. Neither does belonging to a group necessarily generate democratic ideals. On the contrary, being part of a mob that targets others may be driven by a sense of group belongingness but is not a democratic action.

It is the experience of being together among those who are different from us that produces a true public and, through that, a sense of democracy. Actions that are democratic as well as the practices and rituals of democracy are all those that have to produce such spaces. In contrast, one can have an idea of the public that is grounded in mechanisms of institutions, laws and contracts as is more prevalent in some societies, but these are not enough.

Physical spaces that are public spaces are an essential part of the democratic process. The space that is produced as a public space is not a physical space alone. However, many different types of spaces are produced in a society, and a democratic society has to make all these public in the sense defined above. Thus, what I mean by public space includes educational space, cultural space, religious space, among others. Each of these spaces functions undemocratically if, in the name of being public, they function on norms based on exclusion. For example, educational spaces in India today are spaces in which many individuals and groups feel unwelcome. Making this space public is to find ways of accommodating those who are different from the dominant group, those who have not had access to education for countless reasons related to gender, caste and class. So too spaces of health have to be made public in this sense. Similarly, all those spaces in a society that function on exclusion and uniqueness of groups become democratic when such possibilities become part of their everyday functioning.

The argument that a core function of democracy is to produce a notion of the public has a logical consequence: that the policies of reservation as well as schemes to protect minorities are fundamental and necessary democratic processes. In other words, these policies are an expression of the ethics present in this notion of the public. Although these two actions have had significant blowback from the majority community and from those who do not fall under reserved categories, these responses are based on an imperfect understanding of the meaning of democracy. These policies towards the suppressed castes as well as minorities are absolutely essential to any idea of meaningful democracy, since they are ways to produce a sense of the public in which these excluded members also find a place. The reasons for this claim are as follows.

Consider first the marginalized and the excluded. First of all, if they are members of society, then they have an equal share in the public wealth of that society as much as any other member of that society. But their marginalized status—due to various causes such as poverty, caste, gender and religious bias, or belonging to smaller powerless groups—denies them this fundamental right to be a proper shareholder like the others. So any society with a claim to democracy has to find ways to give them their proper share of the public social. Consider the simple example of going to a public park. One might argue that this public space is accessible to anybody. But the very structure of social mobility means that only some have the means to access this public good. A family may not have the money to travel to the park or to buy food when they are there. So the mere existence of an 'open' space is not enough. That is only a condition, but there are other conditions that have to be fulfilled before this space becomes a truly public space.

What is true of the public park is true of every other public good. It is the case today that only a segment of the population has access and benefits from public goods, whether it be health, education, essential services and so on. Those who are kept out have no way of entering the public spaces and take their share of the public wealth unless and until they are given extra support. That is what reservation and special support to minority groups are meant to do. Any society that has the illusion of being democratic has to necessarily take these steps. This is the only path to discovering the social life of democracy. The idea of the public is closely related to notions of truth and freedom. I will discuss these two concepts in the context of democracy in what follows.

5.

DEMOCRACY AND TRUTH

Justice D. Y. Chandrachud, a respected liberal judge of the Supreme Court of India, while delivering the Justice M. C. Chagla Memorial Lecture in 2021, spoke about the relation between truth and democracy.[1] He points out the importance of truth to democracy and he defines democracy as a 'form of governance adopted in order to prevent the tyranny of the few.'[2] He gives some reasons for the importance of truth to uphold democracy: truth produces 'spaces of reason' for decisions, 'instil[s] a sense of public trust in democracies', creates 'a shared "public memory"', the latter particularly important in the case of truth commissions in societies under totalitarian regimes.

He goes on to point out that the relation between truth and democracy has two faces: 'Democracy needs the power of truth to survive. As such, one can consider "speaking truth to power" as a right every citizen must have in a democracy, but equally

---

1 See D. Y. Chandrachud, ' "Democracy Needs Truth to Survive"—Full Text of Justice Chandrachud Speech', *The Print*, 28 August 2021. Available at: https://bit.ly/3zk5WKS (last accessed on 28 July 2022).

2 Chandrachud, 'Democracy Needs Truth', pp. 3–4.

as also the duty of every citizen.'[3] He argues that we need the conceptions of both scientific and moral truths, and suggests a broader conception of truth. He draws upon the Truth and Reconciliation Commission of South Africa and the four different kinds of truth that they defined:

> The first of these was factual or forensic truth, which we would describe as 'scientific' truth since it is determined on the basis of facts and is the most commonly understood definition of 'truth'. However, it is the other three which were extremely peculiar. The second was personal or narrative truth, which was based upon the cathartic benefit of storytelling, where every person who was affected by the apartheid regime could come forward and tell their story in public hearings. The third was social or 'dialogue' truth, which was defined by Justice Albie Sachs of the Constitutional Court of South Africa as 'the truth of experience that is established through interaction, discussion and debate'. The basis of this truth often arose from the dialogue surrounding the work of the Truth Commission, which happened in an entirely public setting. And finally, the fourth was healing and restorative truth, where the Truth Commission offered an acknowledgment of the crimes committed against the survivors by putting the facts collected by them in their proper political, social, and ideological context.[4]

He then draws upon historian Sophia Rosenfeld who identifies three different kinds of truths in democracies. One is by the State, the other by experts such as scientists, and the third kind

---

3 Chandrachud, 'Democracy Needs Truth', p. 7.

4 Chandrachud, 'Democracy Needs Truth', p. 12.

that arises out of 'deliberation and discussion by the citizens' in the public space. He then concludes by pointing out the new challenges to the idea of truth in a post-truth world mediated by technology.

The first point that I will make about these observations is that in our common understanding, truth does not arise explicitly in public discussion of social practices like democracy. But, we can nevertheless notice, in the comments above, the fulcrum on which truth and 'democracy as social life' meet. Chandrachud argues for the importance of truth to democracy because of the nature of 'public spaces', the production of 'public trust' as well as its capacity to produce 'shared memories'. All these are terms that we have discussed earlier where it was seen that they are essential to ideas of the social self and the democratic self. So truth in its relation to democracy is not a cognitive act that is divorced from the social realities but one that is deeply embedded in these realities and structures.

Truth is foundational to democracy. Even if we restrict ourselves to the political act of governing on behalf of the people, it is clear that truth plays an important role in earning the trust of those whom the politicians represent. Representatives are chosen in the hope that their actions will be true to their words and promises. Trust itself is related to truth when trust is understood as a public entity and not as a psychological state. Although a child's trust in her parents is not explicitly based on some notion of truth, nevertheless the constancy in behaviour improves the trust the child has in them. Similarly, in the public domain, there are different expressions of truth that are foundational for an effective democracy.

Of late, truth has become a matter of concern, given the growth of what has been called 'post-truth' politics, and more particularly, the explicit influence of lies in the conduct of politics. Globally, across governments, there is a blatant use of lies in order to justify their actions, most recent of which is Russian president Vladimir Putin's war on Ukraine. Ironically, this is occurring at a time when transparency and access to information have drastically increased due to new technologies. However, one could argue that it is precisely these new technologies that have catalysed the blatant shift to lies because these technologies have diluted truth by producing uncontrollable amounts of 'truths'. It is the sheer volume of facts in the world that allows for the propagation of lies. Blatant lies characterize every political party's claims. What has happened is that we have moved from an analog world where truths were hidden as secrets to a digital world where lies are hidden as truths.

Truth is a complex concept, particularly in the context of human interactions. Firstly, there are many different types of truth—this is not equivalent to the claim about the plurality of truths. Different domains of human action have different ideas of truth. For example, it is firmly believed that truth about the empirical world—the world we sense—is different from the truth that is produced through 'pure' thinking. Truth in mathematics is of a different kind as compared with truth in the empirical sciences, both natural and social. Truths experienced by individuals are different from truths that are accessible to many. Moral truths are of a different kind than factual truths. Although religion is often reduced to beliefs, the effort of theologians of all religions point to the centrality of an idea of truth in religion. Many artists often describe their work in terms of truth. Truth in art is as much valued as truth in the sciences but the nature of this truth is different from that of the factual and the empirical world. What type of truth is of relevance to democracy then? Which theories of truth would make sense to democratic action and a democratic life? If we restrict ourselves to politics, then this is equivalent to asking for the nature of truth in politics. Unless we understand the unique contour of truth in politics, we cannot really make a meaningful analysis of truth and democracy. In exploring this nature of truth in politics, we will recognize that such truths are deeply related to the social life that produces them.

There is one common conceptual problem in all these different domains of truths and it has to do with the articulation or description of truth. If we believe, as many do, that truth is independent of its description through language, then the gap between truth and its linguistic description is a perennial gap that can be exploited to promote lies as truths. This is not a problem merely for politics; it is true for every articulation of truth. Consider the analogy with objects. Objects are real and have an existence independent of how we describe them. Objects are not truthful or not so; it is only statements that we judge as being true or not. In many Indian languages, the word for truth and real are similar and arise from the same root, *sat*. So the real problem about truth arises when we use language and other forms of description of some state of affairs. Even a perception of a table with two fruits can lead to multiple descriptions. First, there can be descriptions in different languages and these descriptions will depend on the conceptual vocabulary of each language. Second, even in one language there are multiple ways of describing the table with two fruits on it. Each description might focus on some particular aspect or might describe new features or add the context and background to this description. All of these descriptions are potentially truthful even though they may be saying different things. If this is the case with a 'simple' perception of a table with two fruits, imagine how much more complicated this gets when more complex events are described!

This is really the crux of the problem. Since I have repeatedly argued that democracy lies in the domain of everyday social life in all its manifestations, then to understand the link between truth and democracy we need to consider the different types of truths in these various domains. If we limit ourselves to politics, then we should be starting with the nature of truth in politics. There is a genuine problem that all of us face today when we talk about truth. It is becoming more and more difficult to find norms of debate, ways of convincing others, of being able to say 'this is how it is'. It is becoming impossible to say anything without being labelled as this or that. This is not merely a problem of identity as many tend to see it. It is more a problem of grasping some notion of truth that is common across domains, as well as the nature of truth and its articulation in public spaces, including politics.

The problem of truth in politics is not new. One could in fact see the emergence of various kinds of political apparatus, including institutions such as parliament, as ways to enforce some norms of truthful action and behaviour. Harold Pinter, in his 2005 Nobel lecture titled 'Art, Truth and Politics', notes that the

> [M]ajority of politicians, on the evidence available to us, are interested not in truth but in power and in the maintenance of that power. To maintain that power it is essential that people remain in ignorance, that they live in ignorance of the truth, even the truth of their own lives. What surrounds us therefore is a vast tapestry of lies, upon which we feed.[5]

---

5 Harold Pinter, 'Art, Truth and Politics', Nobel Lecture, 2005. Available at: https://bit.ly/3SeI5ow (last accessed on 30 July 2022).

Given the perceived view that politics is about power, discussion on truth in politics often revolves around the oft-articulated phrase 'speaking truth to power', a phrase that Justice Chandrachaud also invokes in his memorial lecture discussed above. But phrasing the relation between truth and power in this manner seems to imply that truth and power are independent. However, this need not be the case. In fact, as one might say following Gandhi, power is also derived from truth. We do not have to speak truth to power if truth and power are essentially tied to each other right from the beginning. But the value that this phrase has attained in public discourse perhaps only points to the fact that we live in an age where power has been divorced from truth. Thus, it is possible to claim that an important aspect of democracy is that it would not allow truth and power to be delinked, and every democratic action is one that retains the answerability of each to the other at every stage.

The problem of truth in politics is compounded by the confused understanding of the human individual. Liberal democracies place great value on the individual and democracy has often been reduced to autonomy and choice of individuals in a political system. In such a view, an internal conflict within democracy arises most starkly when confronted by individuals who seem to not act autonomously (such as voting based on group membership to caste and religion or ideologies), or act against their own interests (in choosing leaders who are potentially harmful to their interests), or act in ways that harm others (by choosing candidates based on ideologies of hatred and disrespect), or to go against all norms by accepting blatant lies as truths (this self-delusional practice by individuals in full bloom in contemporary times). So the ideas that have to be understood first before we talk of democracy are questions on the nature of the human individual, the qualities ascribed to, and the ideal norms expected of, the individual. Is the creation of an autonomous, rational individual itself a product of a particular cultural history that has somehow been so valorized but each time finds itself short in the face of human action? Is the remedy a relook at the nature of the individual that is representative of ideas across the world and not just at one moment in an intellectual European history that sustains itself through various forms of political, economic and intellectual power?

To understand the relation between truth and democracy, start with the ambiguous relation that human beings have with truth. We are not always truthful although most of us may be truthful for the most part. In my philosophy workshops with young children, the most common response when we discuss ethics is their view that lying is not really wrong and not always wrong. Qualified lying is seen as a virtue in many cases, including lying to one's parents to escape punishment! Lying is endemic in all our societies, including consumerist economies which are sustained by various mutations of truth. Advertisements always present products in a way that is never 'completely' truthful. Salespeople across the world are not seen as paragons of truth. For example, the 2015 Pew Research Centre report pointed out that politicians received the lowest percentage for honesty compared with businesspeople and others (even the market was seen as more truthful!).[6] Another report, from the McCann Truth Central, with inputs from the US, UK and India in 2012, found that 72 per cent people in these three countries agreed that truth was hard to find in politics and that politicians as a group were seen as the least truthful, in the dubious company of salesmen.[7]

---

6 Pew Research Center, 'Beyond Distrust: How Americans View Their Government', 23 November 2015. Available at: https://pewrsr.ch/3RBMuRx (last accessed on 2 September 2022).

7 McCann Truth Central, 'Truth about Politics', 3 October 2012. Available at: https://bit.ly/3ekD3rk (last accessed on 2 September 2022).

Politicians would presumably take offence at these conclusions. But more importantly, they might actually respond by saying that these numbers are themselves not 'true'! In what sense are they true and not true? Firstly, they are based on a naive understanding of truth. The truth in selling a car and the truths somebody can share about a national policy are two entirely different things. So the question we come back to is this: What is the kind of truth that is characteristic of politics? Since democracy is closely linked to politics, I would say that these responses towards politicians and the relation to truth is a reflection of misunderstanding the nature of both politics and truth.

Hannah Arendt also had a similar moment of doubt about truth and politics after she wrote her Adolf Eichmann reports. She was attacked for a variety of reasons after the publication of her reports on the Eichmann trial in Jerusalem. In response, she wrote an essay which was published in the *New Yorker* in 1967. The reasons for writing the response, she pointed out, were two. One was the question of 'whether it is always legitimate to tell the truth' and the other was as a response to the charges of lies against her, lies about what she wrote and about her facts. Her essay was titled 'Truth and Politics' and it is instructive to note the relation between power and truth that she also evokes:

> No one has ever doubted that truth and politics are on rather bad terms with each other, and no one, as far as I know, has ever counted truthfulness among the political virtues. Lies have always been regarded as necessary and justifiable tools not only of the politician's or the demagogue's but also of the statesman's trade. [...] Is it of the very essence of truth to be impotent and of the very essence of power to be deceitful?[8]

---

8 Hannah Arendt, 'Truth and Politics' in *Between Past and Future Eight Exercises in Political Thought* (London: Penguin, 2006[1968]), pp. 223–59; here, 227–8.

Arendt identifies some essential tensions between truth and politics. She first points out that 'truth seekers' are fine as long as they do not involve themselves in social action. By imparting a virtue to the task of truth seeking, she locates the Platonic distinction between truth seekers and ordinary citizens. She makes a further distinction between rational and factual truths: 'The modern age, which believes that truth is neither given to nor disclosed to but produced by the human mind, has assigned, since Leibniz, mathematical, scientific, and philosophical truths to the common species of rational truth as distinguished from factual truth.' This view is important since, for her, politics is concerned with factual truths and arises as consequences of human interactions. But then such truths are a problem because 'facts and events are infinitely more fragile things than axioms, discoveries, theories—even the most wildly speculative ones— produced by the human mind; they occur in the field of the ever-changing affairs of men.'[9]

Arendt makes an important observation that historically, the problem regarding truth and politics arose as a clash between the philosopher and the citizen, based on philosophy's notion of unchanging truth (or valuing truth as unchanging and eternal) and *opinion* of the citizen. She argues that therefore the opposite of truth was not the category of lie but only opinion, and this leads to the possibility of communication through dialogue (philosophy) and through rhetoric (politics). Therefore, the greatest danger was not in the countering of factual truth through lies but 'reducing' them to opinion once it becomes a public commodity. She reminds us that in earlier times ignorance was seen as worse than lying. We can understand this sentiment today, especially when ignorance is used as a deliberate

---

9 Arendt, 'Truth and Politics', p. 231.

strategy that resists the will to know. In the response to blatant fake news, this attempt to hide within ignorance can be clearly discerned. Denial is another form of ignorance and self-delusion. Lying is different as compared with ignorance or error because lying is deliberate falsehood.

Calling lying a deliberate falsehood is based on a particular conception of autonomous action. The deliberateness picks out the agency of the human actor and this agency is seen as more important than 'falsehood' as such. This is also a reflection of the suspicion that all intellectual traditions have had of the common citizen, as somebody who cannot be trusted. Democracy is based on a principle that citizens have to trust their representatives and those who govern them, but the citizens themselves are never in a position of reciprocal trust by the 'rulers'. This asymmetry in democracy leads to different versions of truth and falsehood for the rulers and ordinary citizens. If the agency is given back to the citizens in terms of their engagement with truth and falsehood (and not just as passive receivers or passive voters), then deliberate falsehood is not just associated with the rulers but with the citizens themselves. We see this all the time in Indian democracy when politicians go to groups and ask for their vote or give them some inducement to vote for them. The question that we need to ask in the context of Asian and African democracies is what theories of truth do they base their lives upon and what notions of autonomy and deliberateness characterizes their actions. By so doing, we can immediately see other possibilities of understanding democracy in these societies.

There is another important point that Arendt makes and this is crucial to the processes of democracy. She locates the problem in the shift from 'rational truth' to opinion as a shift that necessarily happens in the shift from the singular to the plural. Plato's conviction 'that truth can be neither gained nor communicated among the many' privileges the solid reasoning of one's mind to the strength of opinion due to many, and thus converts the problem of truth to the problem of the many, of the 'people/citizens' and of the 'collective'. Thus, truth (based on the one) and politics (based on the many) will always be at odds. Arendt concludes that 'it may be in the nature of the political realm to be at war with truth in all its forms'. While these reflections on truth in the context of politics raise many questions, we should recognize that the problems are as much to do with the concept of truth as what the nature of politics is or should be. Are there other ways of understanding truth in politics? What is the relationship between the nature of truth in politics, particularly democratic politics, and that of truth in everyday life and ordinary human interactions?

Truth, Politics and Democracy

I will begin by listing eight 'minor' arguments on the question of truth in politics.

First, I begin with the contention that there is really no problem even if politics is about lies. Most lies are typically seen as a negation of truth. But if this is the case then the problem about truth is not as serious as one might think. This is because once somebody knows that a particular statement is a lie, then this person knows the truth, because the truth will be that which is the opposite of the lie. Every individual who has the intellectual capacity to vote can figure this out. A liar doesn't have to speak the truth at all; it can be discovered merely by listening to the lie! One might then shift the problem of deciding what a lie is to who is a liar. Considering that most people, as mentioned earlier in this section, think of politicians as liars, this is also not difficult. So lies are not the real problem. However, inferring from a lie is not as simple as inferring from a truth since there could be more than one possibility in this case. Suppose we know that the statement 'This apple is sweet' is true; in this case, we know a particular property of the apple—that it is sweet. Now suppose we know that 'This apple is sweet' is a lie. Then what property of the apple can be inferred? The inference from the lie can be many: the apple could be sour, it could be bitter, it could be spoilt, and so on.

Moreover, one can understand the role of lying differently and not only as deliberate falsehood as Arendt suggests. Even in the case of a 'deliberate falsehood', what is really wrong with it? Sometimes as a teacher I might deliberately give a wrong answer to the class to incite them to think about various alternatives—including the right answer, the way to respond to authority, to question what a teacher says and so on. I am strictly not lying since the deliberateness in creating the falsehood has a different intention. Thus, for lies to have negative connotations as in Arendt's use of 'deliberate falsehood', we have to look for the intentionality behind the deliberateness. There are other examples where deliberate falsehood is actually part of an epistemological enquiry. In modelling in the sciences, one can begin with deliberately easy or contrary assumptions to see what the consequences of that will be. So one might say that there is an epistemic function for lies and perhaps that is the role lying has in politics. If in our ordinary lives we begin with the potential truth of a statement and then test for its veracity, in politics we begin with the assumption that it is a lie and then test for its truth. Thus, lying becomes the core truth of certain political actions. Potential lies as the starting point inspire the act of politics since there is immediate disagreement. Such behaviour is often seen in foreign-policy negotiations where truth is not laid out on the table to start with. Politics is a constant negotiation between the politician and the citizens, as well as between truth and lies.

There is an added complication. The politician embodies the liar paradox except that as a liar when he is saying 'I am not lying' it is different from the usual case of an individual uttering the same statement. That is, the paradox of lying does not manifest as in the liar paradox of a solitary speaker. It is more like this: Consider two politicians, A and B, during an election. A claims that what B says is false, and B claims that what A says is false. Both of them are making this claim to the voters. This situation is not a simple liar paradox but a liar paradox with two agents who say that the other is lying. Interestingly, in this case, A and B are not talking to each other at all. It is not that A is saying B is lying and B is saying A is lying to each other. Both A and B are primarily addressing the voter/citizen and they are asking the voter to decide who is really lying and who is not. This is actually a paradox not for the speakers but for the listeners and is strictly a 'listener paradox'. The listener has to make a judgement on whether A and B are uttering truth or lies when each accuses the other of speaking falsehood.

And this is precisely what I referred to earlier when I mentioned that in politics, lying is a form of negotiation and is not a statement that has to be validated for its truthfulness. As in geopolitics, when the negotiator of one nation begins with a statement, it is not taken at face value by the other team. It is a card that is dealt and has to be interpreted by the other team. When politicians tell an obvious lie, it is not that they do not know that it can be fact-checked. During the 2020 US election campaign, it was amusing to see journalists rushing to give statistics of fact checks for every major speech by the then president and others. Politicians, especially during an election, are not offering truths that need justification through verification. They utter a lie knowing well that it is a lie and that there are many (like the fact checkers) who can show that it is a lie. Then why utter it? It is not that the citizens are fools who will accept everything that the politician tells them. It is not that those who voted for Trump are swayed by the fact checks since that is not the nature of political truth and political lies. Political utterances are only a call for a negotiation, a protracted negotiation. It is a way to open up the spaces of other truths, of more truths. However repugnant this practice of public lying during election campaigns may be, it is repugnant only because there seems to be no stable point from which truth can be judged and labelled as such in human negotiations.

Secondly, one could say that politics is not really about truth anyway because truth is primarily truth of something. The truths of science are the truths of the natural world. Just as science is about the natural world, what is politics really about? In ordinary conversation, we recognize a particular nature of politics when we say, 'He got the job because of politics.' In saying this, we actually understand politics as something much more than mere elections or choosing representatives to govern. The commonly uttered sentiment that 'this is all politics' as a way of expressing that true skills were not the criteria for choice is actually an important statement about what the citizens think of politics. It is not that politics is only about lies; it is also that politics is an invisible domain that cannot be pinned down. When we do not have the exact reasons why somebody was chosen ahead of others, we invoke the term politics. Politics in this sense is a domain with unspecified causal powers.

There is an important lesson in this example. It is that truth in politics is truth about effects and is not restricted to truth in content. Truth in content (truths about facts and propositional truths) is only useful insofar as they produce a truth of effects.

Thus, political truth is not factual knowledge but only a mechanism that is concerned with producing real effects. Therefore, the act of politics lies in the mechanism of *moving from falsity of assertions to truthfulness of effect*. Truth is not used as a legitimization but as a causal entity. This brings it close to pragmatic theories of truth in scientific realism. For example, money is not 'truth' in any sense but it has real effects, including effects on voting. Truth about money is only equal to its effect.

Thirdly, we can understand the role of lying not in opposition to truth but as a particular kind of response. Politics is a domain filled with conspiracy theories, for example. Why? Why are such theories much less in other domains where truth appears, such as in science or mathematics? The very idea of politics catalyses not just conspiracy theories but also psychological explanations as truth makers, such as anger in people, their sense of injustice and so on. Content-based and factual truths are incapable of capturing the complex truths of politics. Citizens respond to the absent space of truth makers by producing other narratives to fill up that space. Perception of political truth largely occurs in attempts to discover it in the domain of the unsaid. Thus, politics demands that the citizen also function as a specialist in that the task of adjudicating truth is left to the ordinary person who is listening to the politician. But if the citizen is asked to adjudicate and validate truths which he or she is incapable of, then there is a recourse to these narratives. But today this act of making the ordinary citizen a specialist has led to great scepticism since it looks like we cannot trust anything any more.

Fourthly, one could say that politics is fundamentally about truth (like other knowledge domains). In this case, we would then have to consider the types of truth that are of relevance to politics as well as questions about the nature of justification in politics, analyse the relation between power and truth as well as the nature of truth in human interactions, which is very different from truths about external realities. This topic is much discussed and I am not convinced by attempts to resuscitate traditional theories of truth within politics.[10] One can more usefully look at other theories of truth that are relevant to politics, particularly the theory of truth as action which I discuss later.

Fifthly, another version of political truth that is actually far closer to the realities of political action is analogous to truth in engineering. Unlike science, where the nature of truth is far more fixed and determined, truths in engineering are produced, literally 'manufactured'. Moreover, they are produced as by-products of conscious actions. The nature of truths in science and engineering are radically different in many cases. In science, truths are about natural phenomena, of an already pregiven universe. But in engineering, truths are those that are amenable to production and manipulation. Political truths are produced and are subject to use, manipulation and application. Truths conform to the expectations of the agents. Arendt anticipates this nature of political truth, although not explicitly in the context of engineering, when she notes that you can make a truth happen in politics, such as the statement that somebody is dead and then you go and kill her.

Sixthly, we can consider the view that politics is actually not about lying and is not about lies. It is only anti-truth. It can speak truth and yet be anti-truth. It needs truth and yet be in a contentious relationship with it. It recognizes that truth cannot be the framework for human negotiations. When something is taken as true then its negotiability conditions decrease. So

---

10 For example, see Jeremy Elkins and Andrew Norris (eds), *Truth and Democracy* (Philadelphia: University of Pennsylvania Press, 2012).

politics is a constant attempt to hold on to truth but, at the same time, also take the *stance* of anti-truth: this is the methodological core of the act of doing politics. Since everything else in our life is based on norms in which truth plays an important role and in which truth functions normatively, we find it difficult to understand politics. For example, in politics, especially in India today, the term 'anti-national' is constantly used against those who are usually critical of the government. The use of 'anti' as opposed to 'not' is important. Politics is not to be seen as not-truth but anti-truth. Politics is anti-truth in the sense that it wants to problematize the notion of truth even while holding on to it as the major medium of discourse. Interestingly, this is most strikingly illustrated in the use of fake news as a political ploy. The labelling of fake is dependent intrinsically on the idea of truth. When something is called fake, there is an underlying suggestion that there is another truth or other truths in contrast to which the fake is defined. Thus, the rhetorical use of fake news is not really about lies but about the nature of truth in politics.

This approach to truth in politics is best illustrated in the act of negotiation. Political action is distinguished by negotiation between agents. The way that this negotiation happens in politics is different from other forms of negotiations. And most crucially, the nature of negotiation when there are differing truth claims captures the problem of the relation between politics and truth. 'Real' truth is not negotiable. It is given and is true. Factual truths which are contingent are dependent but not always negotiable. So one political party might claim that their policies helped the country and the opposition would claim the opposite. The two parties might even give some evidence to support their respective claims but the aim of political discourse is not to come to an agreement but to find ways to refute and reject the evidences supplied by the other. In other words, negotiation is first through rejection, and as in the case of fake news, each assertion is backed by claims of truth. Interpreting this as saying that there are plural and multiple truths is also not always correct. In the conflict between two parties, say A and B, A's claims are in the language of truth and so are B's. But what is special to politics is that A's and B's claims are not adjudicated by each person's version of truth. So the question is to find ways to reconcile A and B politically and not just epistemically.

Seventhly, we can consider yet another possibility. Against what I suggested in the first argument in this list, it may not be possible to derive truth from a lie. Multivalued truths are one example of assertions which cannot be judged to be right or wrong all the time. Moreover, we can consider the view that the truth of a statement is nothing but the conditions under which the statement is true. In politics particularly, this view of truth is far closer to the ground realities of political practice. When somebody questions something as being true, they may not be questioning its facticity but more the conditions under which the assertion is made. This is a particularly powerful way of thinking about truth and multi-valuedness in Jaina logic. I have elsewhere argued that this approach is essential to public reason:

> The Jaina logicians distinguish seven different ways of qualifying an assertion: specifically, they insist that the 'syāt' qualification must be added to assertions. This qualification translated variously as 'maybe', 'under certain conditions', etc., highlights a simple fact that every assertion is true only under certain conditions, including 'obvious' statements like 'this table is brown'. As a consequence, the statement that 'this table is brown' is true under certain conditions, not true under certain

conditions, and perhaps not expressible under other conditions. If we invoke this form of reasoning then we can see how to negotiate a clash of contrary foundational beliefs. When there is such a clash, it is often the case that there are assertions which contradict each other. The inability to deal with these contradictions leads to violent clashes at one end or consolidation of belief at the other. Thus, I would argue that the inability to deal with two contradictory claims must be taken into account when we discuss the nature of questions and answers. The syāt qualification can be a powerful tool to meaningfully engage contradictions since it has the potential to exhibit the conditions under which the assertions of different belief systems are made and sustained. And it is precisely the knowledge of these conditions that constitute critical understanding of our beliefs, opinions and knowledge.[11]

And finally, the question of truth in politics is about a particular quality of politics that deals with the concept of self-abnegation. Along with truths that are associated with negotiation, an important aspect of politics is related to the idea of self-abnegation. Consider the argument that one of the core aims of politics is to legitimize self-abnegation of one's own autonomy. Beginning with this principle, we can see how the other aspects of truth and democratic action follow. Firstly, the self-abnegation that I refer to is the simple observation that we vote of our own volition so that others can rule/govern us. As discussed earlier, a democratic society is one in which all citizens

---

11 See Sundar Sarukkai, 'To Question and Not to Question: That Is the Answer' in Romila Thapar et al., *The Public Intellectual in India* (New Delhi: Aleph, in association with the Book Review Literary Trust, 2015), pp. 41–61; here, p. 54.

have a share in the public wealth. The public domain belongs to all in some measure. When a government takes on the responsibility of governing, what it does is govern this public wealth (not restricted to money) and it does so not only to not misuse the wealth or destroy it but to actually build upon it, thereby making all the citizens wealthier. This is the basic idea that is enshrined *as* democratic practices. So when citizens vote, they give the responsibility of taking care of the public (their) wealth to the politicians. But why should the citizens voluntarily give up their claim to and share of the wealth? What makes them choose some representative to do this job on their behalf?

When citizens vote, they not only voluntarily give up their share of the public wealth but they also give up their autonomy to take decisions on behalf of the public. Voters consciously let others decide on public goods and public ownership. They give away to others the right to be co-owner of public wealth, and take the rights of others when they accept leadership. If one were a politician, how would she convince people when they ask her why they should voluntarily give away what is theirs to her? How is it possible to continuously legitimize this voluntary loss of autonomy?

Politics is about many other things but to *do* politics in a democracy is fundamentally related to this voluntary abnegation. This quality in democracy has an impact on the quality of political truth. It is that the burden of truth is put on individuals who evaluate an utterance and is not really about the person who makes the utterance. In other words, the site of evaluation of truth is not the speaker but the listener, not the politician as such but the voter. The evaluation of truth and falsity is really not about utterances—what is being said by the politician—but about what and how that is heard by the citizens. Thus, the burden of truth is on the individual who has to respond to these utterances. In a real sense, the politician is not forced to speak the truth since the hearer is the one who will carry the burden of adjudicating it. Through this act, the agency of truth is displaced from the politician to the citizen.

In contrast, we can look at science, where truth truly belongs to the domain of specialists. Non-specialists cannot adjudicate the truth of the matter. Scientific truths are merely communicated to the public when they have to be. Many times even that is not done, and there is a huge domain of scientific 'truths' that are lost in the countless amount of literature produced by scientists. More importantly, scientific truths are not negotiated with the public. Political truths by definition are meant to be negotiated; rhetoric is essential to politics primarily for this reason. This means that the burden of truths has to be adjudicated by the citizens—and where they cannot, these truths are held as state secrets. So the fewer state secrets there are, the larger the domain of truths which has to be evaluated by everybody. Thus, in a sense, the price politics pays for self-abnegation of one's will to power as well as to one's wealth is to deny itself the position of being the sole arbitrator of political truths. This is the bargain: my truth for your vote. This is the burden of truth put on each one of the citizens and they cannot run to a specialist to help them decide. The invisible space of politics is produced within our capacity or incapacity to judge something as true.

This space is where an essential element of the ethics of political truth arises when legitimization is itself made democratic. We can now see why the theme of truth is so essential to democracy. Democracy lies not just in casting votes but in creating a citizenry that can evaluate truth claims. Not all citizens will evaluate in the same manner. Some might use different elements in their evaluation. But the primary step in democracy is democratizing this capacity to evaluate. In other words, when citizens give the freedom to politicians to rule them, the politicians give them the freedom to decide on truth claims. This is the trade-off and it is not a simple one. It is indeed a remarkable transaction—just as the citizens expect the politician to uphold their trust, so too does a politician expect the citizens to uphold his or her trust that they will take the trouble to evaluate their claims. How are citizens expected to take on this role? Today, the task of being a democratic citizen in terms of equipping oneself to do this job of legitimizing truths is left in the hands of the media, scholars, journalists and also politicians. When it is said that democracy is about the freedom to disagree, debate and so on, it is because these are the ways by which adjudication of truths are taken away from the hands of specialists and put into the hands of the citizens. But most times these practices are suggested as if they are the end-all of democracy, whereas these practices are just the means to equip citizens to create a public discourse on truths.

Thus, it is reasonable to suggest that the ethics of truth-action and truth-making are the primary qualities of democratic politics. It is important to recognize how this is different from questions of truth in rational discourse. Very often, democracy is supposed to be supplanted by rational discourse, but what is the relation between rationality, with its standard association with truth, justification and evidence, and democracy? The search for truth in science needs methods that are quite different from the practices of truth as related to democratic practice. There is unbridled curiosity, freedom to intervene and manipulate in the natural world, using technologies to control and duplicate natural phenomena in the search for truth in science. This is very different from the actions corresponding to truth in democracy. So what exactly are we to make of the calls for scientific rationality in political democracy? While scientific facts are important in the evaluation of decisions, the rationality of democratic action is quite different as described above. One of the most important differences that we have to note is that the question of ethics in scientific method has often been relegated to the background whereas in democracy it is really at its core.[12]

There is a deep existential theme in this relation between truth and politics. How does truth become part of all of us? Only through politics. We make something political when we raise the question of ethics to truth. Although 'speaking truth to power' is a much-quoted slogan, it is really 'ethically speaking to truth' which is the first step of democracy. When truth becomes a public property, when it is removed from the *agrahara*—any exclusive domain—only then do we have democratic politics. So the idea of politics is not just about negotiation but negotiation about truths we hold, and thus the act of politics attains its significance in the sustained critique of truths that ground human action.

Since negotiation is a process itself based on layers of facts and intentionalities, truths associated with this act are ethical in nature. This analysis of the nature of truth in politics points towards the essential ethical nature of democratic politics. Truths that arise in the act of negotiation are part of a larger class of truths, where truths are understood as action. Two of the best exemplars who defined and understood truth in this manner are Gandhi and Ambedkar. As Farah Godrej points out, Gandhi's idea of truth in terms of political action 'offers a vision of political action that includes the search for truth as integral to political life. Implicit in this vision is also the possibility that nonviolence, understood in a certain way, provides a means to

---

12 On ethics in science, see Sarukkai, 'Science and the Ethics of Curiosity'.

adjudicate among competing truth claims.'[13] For Gandhi, truth lies in action. Truths are not propositions but are intrinsically entwined with action. For Gandhi, ahimsa is understood as an unshakeable truth, and truth and ahimsa are found through each other. Through this approach, Gandhi foregrounds the importance of experiencing truth. Truth is not just an intellectual by-product but one that should be experienced as such. While one may not be able to experience scientific truths, any truth that is political has to have a domain of experience. Thus, the inner voice of conscience, so important in Gandhi's view of life and politics, is itself an experience that has to be cultivated. This experience leads to an action that is true. So in this approach, we can see the inherent tension between truth as action and truth as reflection alone.

Interestingly, Gopal Guru makes a similar point in a comparison between Gandhi and Ambedkar. He notes that for Ambedkar, 'being truthful means an ethical action has to be such that it ultimately leads to the emergence of an ethically/morally stable social order.'[14] To extend this point, one could say that for Ambedkar truthfulness is a truth-performance. We can see this clearly in the case of the politics of untouchability. For both Ambedkar and Gandhi, untouchability in its action-oriented form contains a lived truth that has to be acknowledged, and such a truth cannot be reduced to 'empirical' evidence alone. It is actions themselves that become the unit of truth and not the consequence of an action or the end product of an action or the elements of an action. We could call this the truth-action, in

13 Farah Godrej, 'Nonviolence and Gandhi's Truth: A Method for Moral and Political Arbitration', *Review of Politics* 68(2) (Spring 2006): 287–317; here, p. 288.

14 Gopal Guru, 'Ethics in Ambedkar's Critique of Gandhi', *Economic and Political Weekly* 52(15) (April 2017): 95–100; here, p. 98.

contrast to truth statements. Truth-actions reflect the credo of being true to yourself not through your positions but by your actions. As Guru writes about Gandhi, 'In subordinating oneself, he was not showcasing sacrifice but being more truthful to himself.' Thus, when truth is analysed as a unit of action, then it is possible to recognize that truth can only appear as actions and not as a content of actions. Thus, truth *appears* and is not *found*. It is not surprising that given Gandhi's and Ambedkar's emphasis on truth and actions of truth, the political movement for India's independence was invested enormously in truth-actions of the self.

There are many layers of truth that regulate politics, even in totalitarian governments. Non-democratic regimes have always used, for their political purposes, religious, scientific and technological truths. The link between truth and despotism was understood by Arendt but she didn't explicate the specific nature of truth that is necessary for democracy. This truth is a type of political truth and has the added qualification of truth as particular actions of the self. Thus the domain of truth in democracy is important in its relation to the formation and actions of the democratic self.

6.

DEMOCRACY AND FREEDOM

There is no doubt that freedom has become one of the most important catchwords of contemporary times. Democracy is often associated with the value of freedom. But freedom from what? Freedom to do what? In the context of democracy, we hear about the importance of free speech, free expression, free thought, freedom to imagine, to criticize, to disagree, to dissent, to protest, to dress and eat what we want, to follow one's faith and so on. Almost everything is defined in terms of freedom and freedom itself is most dominantly defined in terms of choice. But what exactly is the relation between the concepts underlying freedom and that of democracy? What is the nature of freedom as far as it pertains to the qualities of democracy, both in the political as well as the everyday sphere?

Free elections exemplify this function of freedom, since in such elections freedom of the individual is expressed in the act of voting for a person of one's choice without coercion. However, this is only a limited sense of freedom since the list of whom one can vote for is limited by many factors outside the individual's control. In most cases, it may be that none of the candidates is worthy of voting for, yet an individual will end up voting for one of them. The constraints on this so-called free-dom are many. To be a candidate one needs a huge amount of money, and it is not a surprise that most people who stand for elections have access to such extraordinary amounts. Given this context, it is really not clear what freedom in voting really amounts to. There are two aspects to consider here: What exactly is the nature of this freedom and how is this related to democracy that is about many things—liberty, equality, frater-nity, self-abnegation, the ethics of representation? One might argue that freedom in voting is the freedom to choose within a rigid system of political parties. Freedom here is not very dif-ferent from freedom in shopping or freedom to choose what one wants to eat at a food court in a mall. There is a measure of free action that is nevertheless regulated by the limitations of what kind of shops and restaurants are present or can be present in the mall. But such a definition of freedom is not really con-ducive to the larger ideals of democracy. For example, in the document on China as a democracy (discussed earlier), there is a description of how citizens have a choice for whom they can vote, although all the candidates may be chosen by the party or by the State. It is clear that given the inherent weakness in the system of voting, China too is able to assert that it is democratic. One might argue that the real freedom in democratic voting is the freedom to have the representatives that people might want. But that is not possible, given the constraints of the system. Moreover, voting based on what people want often gets reduced to what the majority wants, leading to problems of majoritar-ianism that we are seeing across the world today. This situation is complicated by what happens routinely in Indian democracy when money and other inducements are given in exchange for a vote. So whatever illusion of freedom in voting there was now gets lost in this process of voting as a business transaction.

One response is to say that the substantial idea of freedom in voting is not in the act of choosing a candidate. Real freedom in voting is the freedom to hold the elected representative accountable. If this is possible, then it is a democratic quality of freedom. So, in principle, even in the Chinese case, even though voting is only a choice between candidates chosen by the one party, it can still be seen as a democratic action if the person who is elected is answerable to the public. In the Indian case, elected representatives are very rarely accountable for their actions. Rather, since voting itself is largely a transaction, governance becomes yet another transaction. Politicians rule not by being answerable but by finding ways to pay off each of their important constituents. The pay-offs are not just in terms of money; it is also in the form of introducing policies that benefit different splintered groups in society based on caste and religion or promoting some majoritarian ideologies. In what follows, I will explore some thematic ideas around the concept of freedom as it pertains to politics and the social.

Freedom of Speech[1]

Although free speech is often seen as essential to democracy, there is, paradoxically, an inherent tension between free speech and democracy. If free speech is understood merely as the freedom to say what one wants, then that is obviously not conducive to meaningful social behaviour. For example, one can spread falsehood about another in the name of free speech. One can insult, lie, create harm and create hatred through free speech, as is happening now thanks to social media. In these cases, free speech should rightfully be called rumour and gossip. Rumour,

---

1 This section is a more elaborate version of my op-ed article in the newspaper *The Hindu* titled 'When Free Speech Is Truly Free', 22 March 2019.

gossip, fake news and deliberate lying can be hidden under the guise of free speech. These are 'speech' with an ulterior motive. To call these free speech is a mistake.

Just as asking what is the freedom present in voting, we can ask a similar question as to what is really free in free speech. Is it the freedom to say what one wants? In reality, we cannot say all that we want because of various constraints: of grammar, the set of words that are available, set of concepts that are unique to different languages, the context from which we are speaking and so on. Even the sounds that we can make (which is the first unit of language) are constrained by the structure of our mouth and vocal cords. Philosophers have long pointed out that what we perceive is constrained by the limitations of our senses and what we cognize is constrained by our cognitive structures. Our speech is also socially constrained by the people around us and by the larger society. We do not always speak what we want.

Like voting, free speech is only free within a given set of constraints. While there will always be situations where speech transcends some of these constraints, particularly social and political constraints, most often it is only a reflection of what is allowed. There is also another important form of constraint, namely, self-constraint. We often stop ourselves from saying what we want to, both in personal and professional conversations. Most people do this because they recognize that often there is a cost to speech. There is a price to be paid for what we speak. Being honest and outspoken is not always a virtue, especially when the consequences are undesirable. Thus, both due to the nature of sound and language, as well as the control one imposes on what one speaks, it could be said that speech in general is always accompanied by a significant amount of the unspoken.

It is often mistakenly argued that the essence of free speech is the freedom to say what one wants. Actually, when free speech is invoked in the context of everyday discourse, it is more about speech which is free, which comes with no cost. Free speech is actually a demand to be able to speak without having to pay any price for it. It is literally like getting a 'free gift'. However, whether one pays a price or not is *not* in the hands of the person who is speaking. The speaker cannot always predict the consequences of their speech. Whatever be the case, paying the price for speaking something is outside the control of the speaker. It is ironic to note that at a time in our history when free speech is much valorized, there are also growing restrictions on what one can write in the name of identity and political correctness.

If the structure of free speech is understood in this manner, then it is not really about what a person utters or writes. Rather, free speech only describes the conditions under which others are not allowed to take offence and intimidate the speaker/writer. Thus, the significant meaning of freedom in 'free speech' is not the freedom of the speaker to say what she wants, nor is it about the freedom of the receiver to react in the way he wants. It is not about positive freedom but is more a set of constraints on others in order to enable the speaker to say what they want. The demand for the right to free speech is essentially a demand for the right to not allow individuals, groups or the government to restrict what an individual can say. The most important consequence of the idea of free speech is that it shifts the responsibility of free speech from the speaker/writer to those who hear/read this person. *Thus, the function of free speech is not to liberate the individual but to liberate the society around the individual in order to let the individual speak what she wants.*

But does this mean that any individual, in the name of free speech, can say what they want or slander another through falsehood? If slandering an individual is not acceptable, then can they slander a government or a politician? In this context, it is important to remember that the most effective punishment against free speech comes from governments. We have repeatedly seen how governments (particularly in India) often use the charge of sedition to stop people from expressing criticism in the public space. From the definition of free speech that I discussed above, one can say that the freedom to slander a person is not about what one says but about the conditions that will support the person who is slandering another. While some may agree that it is not free speech to purposefully slander a person, most would agree that an important function of democracy is to be able to say what the citizens want about the government. Such criticism is not just a right, it is more a duty of democratic societies. In a true democracy, there is nothing that can be considered as slandering the government, even if a criticism may be wrong and unjustified. This is because the contract between the voter and the voted-for is a contract that demands accountability from the person who is voted to power. Thus, free speech is a tool to create the conditions for democracy to work. It cannot be reduced to the act of speaking or writing what an individual 'desires/wants' but is intrinsically tied to the accountability expected of the person towards whom free speech is directed.

The true power of free speech lies in its capacity to make those in power accountable to those who do not have power. It is a means to make those in power answerable and is not really about freedom of individuals. It is a set of conditions that allows the act of speech to not be penalized. The price that people demand for making somebody govern on their behalf (the elected leaders) is the enabling of conditions that let them say what they want about them, not as individuals but as political leaders. So free speech is protected insofar as it is within the contract of answerability, that is, if it falls under topics on which a politician is answerable to the people. True free speech covers only those acts of speech that speak against power, and keep those in power accountable. It thus safeguards a most cherished democratic principle. Free speech by itself is not the essence of democracy but is the means by which any democracy can be sustained. The importance of free speech is diluted when it is used to derive personal benefit or cause harm or do so in situations which are not about power. Speech, in its task of keeping check on power, has to be subsidized and made free by those in power.

Free speech in other domains has to be seen through this framework. One cannot sit among friends or within a family and invoke this idea of free speech that is necessary for the political space. A child cannot assert that it can say what it wants within a family under the guise of 'free speech' since the notion of freedom within a family is different from other spaces. This does not mean that every individual within a family cannot say what they 'want'. All we can conclude is that it is not easy to transfer ideas of free speech in political democracy to democratic practice within families or even within the social world. We have to firstly formulate the correct meaning of freedom in these spaces before we can understand the nature of free speech in other domains.

Freedom to Dissent[2]

Disagreeing with each other is a fundamental human trait. There is not a single individual who does not disagree with someone or other all the time. Philosophers argue that a baby meaningfully attains its sense of the self—its recognition of 'I' and the concept of 'mine'—when it first begins to say 'no'. At a primordial level, we become individuals only through this act of stating our disagreement. Dissent characterizes everything humans do and

2 This section is an edited version of my op-ed article in the newspaper *The Hindu* titled 'The Nature of Dissent', 4 September 2018.

in all domains such as the family, workplace, society and the political arena.

Dissent has an everyday life. It is through different forms of dissenting that relationships are established with those we engage with or relate to. It would be an impoverished human existence if human experience consisted only of agreements, since disagreements are an essential way of learning. The real meaning of the 'social' is about learning to live with those who disagree with each other and not only with those who agree with everything one does. Dissent is so ingrained in humans that others are not really needed to disagree since every individual constantly disagrees with themselves. Each one argues with their own selves all the time as if each of them is actually an individual made up of many selves. The act of thinking captures this process of dissenting with oneself. Thinking is most commonly experienced as a form of dialogue within oneself and most often decision making involves arguing with oneself. Thinking gets its cognitive power because through thinking, individuals are able to dissent with themselves. Thus, when dissent is stifled within one's own minds, thinking stops.

Dissenting, even with oneself, makes the individual function like a social system. The social is present within the individual every time the individual dissents not only because of the multiple selves that one talks to but also because of the use of language to dissent. Language is a socially produced entity and derives its meaning through social use. When an individual speaks, she is speaking not her thoughts alone but, because she uses the language of others, she is also 'speaking others'. Since dissent has this sociality associated with it, the real problem is not dissent but silent assent. Assenting too is cognitively important because it consolidates and builds on thoughts that one has, but agreeing collectively all the time is really not the existential characteristic of a human being but only that of a 'bonded mind'. Just as a baby attains its sense of self through dissent, so too does a society get its own identity by learning to dissent, thereby leading to the conclusion that a society and a nation will have a stronger identity only through forms of dissenting. In fact, a social is formed only through differences and the glue is disagreement as much as agreement between individuals.

A mature society is one which has the capacity to manage dissent since members of a society will always disagree with each other on something or the other. Democratic societies are the best of the available models in managing dissent with the least harmful effect on the dissenter. This is the true work of democracy; elections and voting are the means to achieve this. The essence of democracy is to be found in the method it uses to deal with dissent, which is through discussion and debate, along with particular ethical norms. A democratic society manages dissent by trying to make individual practices of dissent into social practices. Academia and research are two important activities where dissent is at the core. No society has survived without making changes to what was present earlier. New knowledge and new ways of understanding the world, for good or bad, has always been part of every society. Science, in its broadest meaning, is not possible without dissent since it is by finding flaws with the views of others that new science is created. No two philosophers agree on one point, and no two social scientists are in perfect harmony with each other's thoughts. Artists are constantly breaking boundaries set by their friends and peers. Buddha and Mahavira were dissenters first and philosophers next. The Ramayana and Mahabharata are filled with stories of dissent and responsible ways of dealing with it. Dissent is not just about criticism; it is also about showing new perspectives.[3]

3 For more, see Romila Thapar, *Voices of Dissent: An Essay* (London: Seagull Books, 2020).

Dissent exemplifies the ethical imperative present in the foundational principles of democracy. It is not just a pragmatic tool for better democracy but is the conceptual glue that holds the logic of democracy together. There are fundamental ethical principles associated with dissent. One of the most important of these is non-violence, a principle that supplies the ethical backbone of social dissenters like Gandhi and Ambedkar, as well as of so many civil rights movements today. Another important ethical principle of dissent is that of protecting the right to dignified existence of the poor and the marginalized of a society. These two principles raise dissent above the category of complaints or entitlement. Entitlement as dissent has no ethical force to it since it is based on the desires of an individual and meant for the benefit of the individual. Dissent, as ethical, is social and social dissent is necessary for all those who are oppressed and are marginalized.

It follows therefore that the worse-off in a society have greater right to dissent and protest even when the more privileged may not agree or sympathize with that dissent. Thus, when the voices of dissent from the oppressed and the marginalized are heard, then it is ethically incumbent upon others who are better off to give them greater space and greater freedom to dissent. More importantly, the function of any democracy is to enable the conditions and space necessary for these groups to disagree and dissent with what the other segments of society do to them. This is a necessary consequence of the fundamental ethical essence of democracy that I discussed earlier—that the only meaningful idea of democracy has to be based on governance for the well-being of the worst-off in society. Those who are better off act immorally when they sit in the comfort of their homes and abuse those who fight for the rights of the poor and the oppressed. As dissent is a tool for the poor to protest, so also is it essential for groups that are minorities in majority-ruled states. So dissent is not just saying no—it is about saying no to what many others say yes to.

An important lesson from the analysis of what is free in free speech and the freedom to dissent is that freedom is really not about individual choice or even promotion of individual 'rights'. Freedom, as functional and relevant to democracy, is primarily the freedom for an individual to act so that others may become freer. Freedom is only partly located within the individual, and the individual is always an incomplete agent of free action. The genesis of this argument lies in the very nature of freedom and the impossibility of defining it without in opposition to something else. This idea of dissent is not restricted to the political space alone. Dissenting among friends or within families is also related to these qualities of freedom and dissent.

The Problem with Freedom

This analysis of the idea of freedom in a society, and in relation to democracy, already indicates a major misconception about the centrality of freedom in democracy. Most importantly, the idea of freedom as choice given to each and every individual is quite at odds with a meaningful idea of a society. While individualism as a model of society is conceivable, the question is whether such a society can be democratic as a social form of life. Even individualism as a system needs a particular kind of society to enable the functioning of this group of individuals who can retain their identity as individuals. For this to happen, different anonymous structures replace the role of social interactions and this leads to the excessive emphasis on institutions in some Western democracies. But in societies where individualism as a social model is not feasible or even desirable, the idea of freedom and its relation to democracy has to be rethought. Moreover, freedom as a concept is as dispersed and plural as most other concepts. Although we invoke 'freedom' across all domains as if it means the same thing, the meaning of freedom depends on the context in which it is used. Thus, freedom for the individual is different from freedom for a nation, for a majority group, for a minority, for and within families, and for institutions.

For example, consider the difference between the meanings of freedom for an individual and for a nation. In the case of India, the nation attained independence from the British and thus became 'free'. But what does it mean to say that a nation is 'free'? Freedom for the individual is most often understood as the freedom to do what one wants, to act without constraints. But we are forever acting with various constraints—physical, social, legal and moral ones, for example. Today, freedom for individuals has mostly been reduced to choice, to the capacity to be able to choose. The exemplar of freedom today has become consumer choice.

Freedom for the nation is not a freedom of choice. It is not freedom for the nation to do what it wants. Often, the nation is mistakenly equated with the government in power. Freedom for the nation cannot become freedom for the government in power to do what it wants. What then is the nature of freedom for a nation? The fundamental task of a government in a free nation is to provide freedom for its citizens. That is the primary mean- ing of a free society. What kind of freedom can it provide for its citizens? The most fundamental freedoms that a nation has to provide its people include freedom from poverty, freedom to access basic amenities like food and drinkable water, freedom for children to be able to go to schools and enjoy learning, freedom for people to access basic health facilities and freedom from fear. Getting freedom from the colonizers is not the only meaning of freedom for a nation. The absence of fear is the definition of political freedom. A nation is free only when it produces a society where its citizens can live without fear of being victimized or persecuted for ideological reasons. Thus, it is important to understand the nature of freedom before exploring its relation to democracy. I believe that one aspect of the relation between democracy and freedom that has not been emphasized enough is the relation to labour. To understand this point, I will begin with an important work on freedom and slavery by Orlando Patterson.[4]

Patterson sets out to understand how freedom has become one of the most cherished values of the Western world. He notes that 'today freedom stands unchallenged as the supreme value of the Western world . . . [it] is also the central value of Christianity: being redeemed, being freed by, and in, Christ, is the ultimate goal of all Christians.' He attempts to understand why this concept attained such value in the West and surprisingly argues that the concept of freedom as value was never produced in the non-Western world: 'For most of human history, and for nearly all of the non-Western world prior to Western contact, freedom was, and for many still remains, anything but an obvious or desirable goal.'[5]

His answer as to why he locates freedom within the West is as striking. He argues that the idea of freedom arose from the experience of slavery. He attempts to show that freedom came to be valued 'as a result of their experience of, and response to, slavery or its recombinant form, serfdom, in their roles as masters, slaves, and nonslaves.'[6] Although slavery was universal, freedom did not attain the value it did elsewhere, as in the Greek

---

4 Orlando Patterson, *Freedom, Volume 1: Freedom in the Making of Western Culture* (New York: Basic Books, 1992).

5 Patterson, *Freedom*, pp. ix–x.

6 Patterson, *Freedom*, p. xiii.

and Roman world and in Christianity, due to the social structures associated with slavery. For him, the origin of the idea of freedom itself arose from slaves as it was their response to the experience of being slaves. To understand why freedom did not become a value in the non-West, Patterson suggests that there are different types of freedom: personal, sovereignal, and civic freedoms. Personal freedom is the freedom to do as one wishes 'insofar as one can' whereas sovereign freedom is the power to do what one pleases independent of the wishes of others. The third type, civic freedom, is the freedom to be part of a community and participate in it to the full. His point is that although desire for personal freedom was there in all societies, it 'never became a value of any importance in any of these societies' because a value is produced normatively by a group of persons in a society and slaves were never organized enough to create such normative values.[7] Although there is much that can be contested in his comments on personal freedom and freedom as value in non-Western societies, this is not the place, since I am interested in pointing to an important sociological formulation of freedom that becomes particularly necessary in understanding freedom in the context of democracy.

We can extend Patterson's argument to all domains where freedom becomes a value. For example, freedom is an important value in science and in other academic disciplines. Freedom as value becomes essential to the idea of knowledge in modernity and in modern disciplines. In fact, 'academic freedom' is itself an important term which has often been used to argue for liberal policies in academics. But if the creation of a value for freedom is always accompanied by a background condition of slavery, then we can consider the possibility that even in the domains of science and academics in general, there is a background

---

7 Patterson, *Freedom*, p. 35.

condition of repression of some kind. In the case of science, I believe that it is reasonable to argue that Nature takes on the image of a slave. Modern science is possible only when Nature is enslaved, when it is able to be put under the dictates of the human master. Thus, it is not surprising that modern science first begins with changing the meaning of Nature so as to allow experiments, intervention and exploitation of it. Nature is the figure of the slave for science and it is Nature that is now fashioned in the image of a slave so that there is freedom to 'study' it and produce knowledge about it. For a discipline like anthropology, the freedom to study other cultures is predicated on the image of a slave that is imposed on the native/other.[8] The notion of freedom is essential for anthropology since there is an implicit assumption of the freedom of studying another, the freedom to publish descriptions and theories of people who are 'studied'—but all these are freedoms with constraints. This freedom as value is possible only within a master–slave relation where the scholar is the master who writes about others in the image of a slave, who can never be in the position of the master.

The point that should interest us is this: How does freedom attain the normative value it does in democracy? What specific ideas of freedom are invoked here? Is it that the high value ascribed to freedom in democracy necessarily needs a domain of 'slaves' to sustain it? I would suggest that it is 'We, the People' who do this job of being the subordinated but at the same time being presented as the most important value of democracy. 'We, the People' is always less than the people who govern and who are elected by them. Democracy in this model is based on the view that people don't have the capacity to govern by themselves

8 For other themes related to ethics and anthropology, see James Laidlaw, *The Subject of Virtue: An Anthropology of Ethics and Freedom* (Cambridge: Cambridge University Press, 2013).

or by all of them collectively. The ordinary, collective people cannot understand the complexities of this democracy so scholars, politicians and bureaucrats will do this job. A democratic society is now constructed out of hierarchies but is based on the claim of the equality of all. Nothing is farther from the truth. 'We, the People' are not at the same level as the rulers. They are not at the same level as the scholars and analysts. Only some are trained for these positions—that is what education does. Talking about freedom in a democracy is to be silent about the inequality in its foundational concept of 'We, the People'. There is no 'We, the People', to uphold democracy. There is no coherent collection of people, no equality in any sense of the term that binds the people together as one people. Individual freedom by those who can afford this freedom replaces this missing idea at the very heart of democracy.

The critique of freedom is intimately related to the question of labour which was discussed in detail earlier. Freedom for an individual is socially produced; it is not a state that arises 'naturally' from within the individual. It is produced as an idea and it is also produced materially. Children learn the concept of freedom in reference to the objects of freedom. First, these objects are those that are denied to them like sweets they may want to eat. The desire for freedom is developed through the recognition of constraints that they think can be broken. Skipping school is an 'object' of freedom and this is a freedom that breaks constraints. Individual freedom is both freedom-from and freedom-towards. But in general these acts of freedom are always in relation to the larger society around the individual. Wanting freedom is very different from getting it, whether it is getting away from the constraints or getting the object one desires. Most of us live with some chains always around us. It is the recognition of these chains that even makes one desire freedom. But how do we recognize the chains around us, some of them visible and many invisible? And even when we recognize these chains, how do we get out of them? Here is where the role of the social becomes visible. An individual's recognition of the constraints as well as the factors leading to the constraints are produced socially. The social plays a double role in this relation with freedom: it produces constraints on an individual and it also produces the awareness that one is in chains.

While there are many other factors of the social that are needed for this recognition (including language), there is one factor that is essential to achieving the freedom that is desired. And this factor is that of labour. It is the social organization of labour that produces most of the freedoms that individuals desire. One way to express this is by saying that freedom is produced by the slavery of labour: Sanal Mohan's argument that caste should be seen in terms of slavery shows this explicit connection between caste, freedom and slavery.[9] A friend once remarked that after many years of working and establishing her career, she recognized that it was the possibility of getting labour to take care of the house and children that made it possible for her to be 'free'. An individual who wants to have the freedom to buy something or to travel needs different types of labour to support it, such as labour to make the travel possible or factory workers who produce the commodity one wants. The dependence of our freedom on other people's labour is most often forgotten and remains invisible primarily because this dependence is reduced to a financial transaction. We pay for the objects we desire, we pay for the travel and so on. And since individuals pay for this labour, they come to believe that the objects of freedom are products of their own

9 See Sanal Mohan, *Modernity of Slavery: Struggles against Caste Inequality in Colonial Kerala* (New Delhi: Oxford University Press, 2015).

effort. Money and our transactional economy converts the social condition of labour into a purely economic one, thereby producing the illusion that freedom is really about being free and as something to do purely with an individual.

As discussed above, notions of freedom need a condition of slavery, and this is very clearly manifested in the way labour is configured today. The labour system is such that the labourers who produce objects of freedom are rarely able to afford them. Factory workers building cars will not be able to buy the cars they manufacture. In India today, one of the biggest-growing sectors is the construction sector. This desire to have houses, to be free of the constraint of living in rented accommodations, is made possible only because of a huge number of daily-wage earners who are in this profession. Very large numbers of these workers are migrant labourers, who travel to various places to build houses that cannot even feature in their imagination. Freedom as value is only for those who can afford the labour that can produce that freedom for them. In other words, the freedom that is invoked by the urban and the rural rich needs the subordinated to be the rural, the uneducated, the daily labour, the migrant, the poor, the dalit.

There is an important implication of understanding this deeper meaning of freedom: freedom is not a 'right' for all in the same manner. If freedom can ever be taken as a 'right', it can only be so for the oppressed, for those who are hierarchically lower in society due to reasons of gender, caste and class. Freedom for all can be ethically meaningful only when seen in the context of the oppressed. Freedom for an individual can only be in relation to what is freedom for another, for all. And if there are subjugated groups in a society, then liberty of any individual can be guaranteed and protected only to the extent of liberty granted to the subjugated in a society.

So what really is the nature of freedom that is essential to a democratic society? I began with Ambedkar's call to recognize that democracy is not a form of government but a form of society. We have considered the conceptual terrain needed to build on this insight and to explore the possibility of democracy as a form of social life. We also noticed that the phrase 'We, the People' is a problematic term as far as democracy is concerned. But I want to come back to this phrase to recover a notion of freedom that is relevant to democracy. Individual freedom cannot be privileged in democracy because it goes against the centrality of the collective, the people. Privileging the individual in any manner as part of democracy is contradictory to the internal logic of democracy. Thus, the only sense of freedom that is possible in a democratic vision is collective freedom, a freedom that can only be for 'the People' and not for the privileged individuals within this collective. This is a freedom that cannot be reduced to the whims and fancies of individuals. If democracy, unlike other political and social systems that are explicitly hierarchical and exclusionary, has any pretensions that all the people in a democracy have the same 'value', then it has to find ways to produce collective values and not reduce them to values associated with the individual. For this to happen, it is necessary to begin with the collective and the social as the basic unit from which individuals are produced. The only way that we can regroup 'the People' as one entity is by understanding democracy as a way of social life and not as a particular type of political practice. It is the recognition of this social life of democracy as a lived, experiential and moral domain which guarantees Ambedkar's notions of liberty, equality and fraternity.

Paradoxically, this can be done only by investing individuals with certain types of power. Most importantly, by producing a democratic self in each one of us. This democratic self is not only infused with the qualities of liberty, equality and fraternity; it is also one that recognizes the fundamental impulse of democracy as actions that are always geared to make the worse-off better and to make others freer or as free as itself. It is this collective action by each one of us as individuals who function democratically in every action of ours—inside our homes, institutions and public spaces—that will make democracy a meaningful public good. It is only by living democratically in our everyday lives that we can make democracy a form of social life. This form of democracy is the only viable future for human societies.

REFERENCES

ALAM, Javeed. *Who Wants Democracy?* Hyderabad: Orient Longman, 2006.

AMBEDKAR, Bhimrao R. 'Riddles in Hinduism', in *Writings and Speeches, Volume 4* (Vasant Moon ed.). Mumbai: Education Department, Government of Maharashtra, 1989, pp. 282–3.

————. *Writings and Speeches, Volume 13* (Vasant Moon ed.). Mumbai: Education Department, Government of Maharashtra, 1994.

ARENDT, Hannah. 'Truth and Politics', in *Between Past and Future Eight Exercises in Political Thought*. London: Penguin, 2006 [1968], pp. 223–59.

CHAKRABARTY, Dipesh. '"In the Name of Politics": Democracy and the Power of Multitude in India'. *Economic and Political Weekly* 40(30) (23–29 July 2005): 3293–301.

CHANDHOKE, Neera, and Rajesh Kumar. 'Indian Democracy: Cognitive Maps', in K. C. Suri and Achin Vanaik (eds), *Political Science, Volume 2: Indian Democracy*. New Delhi: Oxford Scholarship Online, 2013, pp. 17–52.

CHANDRACHUD, D. Y. '"Democracy Needs Truth to Survive"—Full Text of Justice Chandrachud Speech'. *The Print*, 28 August 2021. Available at: https://bit.ly/3zk5WKS (last accessed on 28 July 2022).

CHATTERJEE, Partha. *I Am the People: Reflections on Popular Sovereignty Today*. New York: Columbia University Press, 2020.

CHINA STATE COUNCIL INFORMATION OFFICE. 'China: Democracy That Works'. *XinhuaNet*, 4 December 2021. Available at: https://bit.ly/-3RyRWFl (last accessed on 12 July 2022).

CONGRESSIONAL RESEARCH SERVICE. 'Government Expenditures on Defense Research and Development by the United States and Other OECD

Countries: Fact Sheet'. Congressional Research Service, 28 January 2020. Available at: https://bit.ly/3qrIHe5 (last accessed on 2 September 2022).

DEWEY, John. *The Middle Works of John Dewey, 1899–1924; Volume 9: 1916, Democracy and Education* (Jo Ann Boydston ed.). Carbondale and Edwardsville: Southern Illinois University Press, 1980.

ELANGOVAN, Arvind. ' "We the People?": Politics and the Conundrum of Framing a Constitution on the Eve of Decolonisation' in Udit Bhatia (ed.), *The Indian Constituent Assembly: Deliberations on Democracy.* London: Routledge, 2018, pp. 10–37.

ELKINS, Jeremy, and Andrew Norris (eds). *Truth and Democracy.* Philadelphia: University of Pennsylvania Press, 2012.

GEETHA, V., and S. V. Rajadurai. *Towards a Non-Brahmin Millennium: From Iyothee Thass to Periyar.* Kolkata: Stree-Samya, 1998.

GODREJ, Farah. 'Nonviolence and Gandhi's Truth: A Method for Moral and Political Arbitration'. *Review of Politics* 68(2) (Spring 2006): 287–317.

GRAY, Emily. ' "Of the People, By the People, For the People": The Implications of Covenantal Union for the Legitimacy of Secession in the United States'. New Haven, CT: Department of Political Science, Yale University, 2013. Available at: https://bit.ly/3RomuK7 (last accessed on 9 July 2022).

GURU, Gopal. 'Ethics in Ambedkar's Critique of Gandhi'. *Economic and Political Weekly* 52(15) (April 2017): 95–100.

——. 'Liberal Democracy in India and the Dalit Critique'. *Social Research* 78(1) (2011): 99–122.

——, and Sundar Sarukkai. *Experience, Caste and the Everyday Social.* Delhi: Oxford University Press, 2019.

——, and Sundar Sarukkai. *The Cracked Mirror: An Indian Debate on Experience and Theory.* Delhi: Oxford University Press, 2012.

KAUFMANN, Laurence. 'Social Minds', in Ian C. Jarvie and Jesus Zamora-Bonilla (eds), *The SAGE Handbook of the Philosophy of Social Sciences.* London: Sage, 2011, pp. 153–80.

KOLGE, Nishikant, and N. Sreekumar. 'Towards a Comprehensive Understanding of Gandhi's Concept of Swaraj: Some Critical Thoughts on Parel's Reading of Swaraj' in Siby K. Joseph and Bharat Mahodaya (eds), *Reflections on Hind Swaraj.* Wardha: Institute of Gandhian Studies, 2010, pp. 171–93.

LAIDLAW, James. *The Subject of Virtue: An Anthropology of Ethics and Freedom*. Cambridge: Cambridge University Press, 2013.

LINCOLN, Abraham. Address delivered at Gettysburg, Pennsylvania, 19 November 1863. Available at the Library of Congress, Washington DC: https://bit.ly/3KJpQ7m (last accessed on 2 September 2022).

MCCANN TRUTH CENTRAL. 'Truth about Politics'. 3 October 2012. Available at: https://bit.ly/3ekD3rk (last accessed on 2 September 2022).

MINISTRY OF SCIENCE & TECHNOLOGY, GOVERNMENT OF INDIA. 'Research and Development Statistics 2019–20'. December 2020. Available at: https://bit.ly/3Rgr6Bh (last accessed on 2 September 2022).

MOHAN, Sanal. *Modernity of Slavery: Struggles against Caste Inequality in Colonial Kerala*. New Delhi: Oxford University Press, 2015.

MUKHERJEE, Arun P. 'B. R. Ambedkar, John Dewey, and the Meaning of Democracy'. *New Literary History* 40(2) (2009): 345–70.

OXFAM INDIA. 'Inequality Kills: India Supplement 2022'. 17 January 2022. Available at: https://bit.ly/3uLr9fc (last accessed on 12 July 2022).

PAREL, Anthony J. 'Introduction: Gandhian Freedoms and Self-Rule' in Anthony J. Parel (ed.), *Gandhi, Freedom, and Self-Rule*. New York and Oxford: Lexington Books, 2000, pp. 1–24.

PATTERSON, Orlando. *Freedom, Volume 1: Freedom in the Making of Western Culture*. New York: Basic Books, 1992.

PEW RESEARCH CENTER. 'Beyond Distrust: How Americans View Their Government'. 23 November 2015. Available at: https://pewrsr.ch/3RBMuRx (last accessed on 2 September 2022).

PINTER, Harold. 'Art, Truth and Politics'. Nobel Lecture, 2005. Available at: https://bit.ly/3SeI5ow (last accessed on 30 July 2022).

REDDY, Sanjay. 'A Rising Tide of Demands: India's Public Institutions and the Democratic Revolution' in Devesh Kapur and Pratap B. Mehta (eds), *Public Institutions in India: Performance and Design*. New Delhi: Oxford University Press, 2005, pp. 457–75.

SARUKKAI, Sundar. *JRD Tata and the Ethics of Philanthropy*. London and New York: Routledge, 2020.

———. 'Science and the Ethics of Curiosity'. *Current Science* 97(6) (2009): 756–67.

———. 'To Question and Not to Question: That Is the Answer' in Romila Thapar et al., *The Public Intellectual in India*. New Delhi: Aleph, in association with the Book Review Literary Trust, 2015, pp. 41–61.

————. 'Voice and the Metaphysics of Protest'. *Postcolonial Studies* 24(1) (2021): 4–10.

————. *What Is Science?* Delhi: National Book Trust, 2012.

SHAPIN, Steven. 'The Way We Trust Now: The Authority of Science and the Character of the Scientists' in Pervez Hoodbhoy, Daniel Glaser and Steven Shapin (eds), *Trust Me: I Am a Scientist*. London: British Council, 2004, pp. 42–63.

SHETH, D. L. *At Home with Democracy: A Theory of Indian Politics*. Singapore: Palgrave Macmillan, 2018.

STROUD, Scott. 'Pragmatist Riddles in Ambedkar's "Riddles of Hinduism"'. *Forward Press*, 1 June 2019. Available at https://bit.ly/3Q2sfME (last accessed on 20 June 2022).

SURI, K. C. 'India's Democracy—An Exception or a Model?' in K. C. Suri and Achin Vanaik (eds), *Political Science, Volume 2: Indian Democracy*. New Delhi: Oxford Scholarship Online, 2013, pp. 1–16.

TAYLOR, Charles. 'The Meaning of Secularism'. *The Hedgehog Review* 12(3) (Fall 2010): 23–34.

THAPAR, Romila. *Voices of Dissent: An Essay*. London: Seagull Books, 2020.